Visual Thought in Russian Religious Philosophy

This book considers a movement within Russian religious philosophy known as "full unity" (*vseedinstvo*), with a focus on one of its main representatives, Pavel Florensky (1882–1937). Often referred to as "the Russian Leonardo," Florensky was an important figure of the Russian religious renaissance around the beginning of the twentieth century. This book shows that his philosophy, conceptualized in his theory of the icon, brings together the problem of the "religious turn" and the "pictorial turn" in modern culture, as well as contributing to contemporary debates on religion and secularism.

Organized around the themes of full unity and visuality, the book examines Florensky's definition of the icon as "energetic symbol," drawing on St. Gregory Palamas, before offering a theological reading of Florensky's theory of the pictorial space of the icon. It then turns to Florensky's idea of space in the icon as Non-Euclidean. Finally, the icon is placed within wider debates provoked by Bolshevik cultural policy, which extend to current discussions concerning religion, modernity, and art.

Offering an important contribution from Russian religious philosophy to issues of contemporary modernity, this book will be of interest to scholars of religious philosophy, Russian studies, theology and the arts, and the medieval icon.

Clemena Antonova is research director of the "Eurasia in Global Dialogue" programme, Institute for the Human Sciences, Vienna, Austria, and author of *Space, Time, and Presence in the Icon: Seeing the World with the Eyes of God*.

Routledge Focus on Religion

Amoris Laetitia and the Spirit of Vatican II
The Source of Controversy
Mariusz Biliniewicz

Muslim and Jew
Origins, Growth, Resentment
Aaron W. Hughes

The Bible and Digital Millennials
David G. Ford, Joshua L. Mann, and Peter M. Phillips

The Fourth Secularisation
Autonomy of Individual Lifestyles
Luigi Berzano

Narratives of Faith from the Haiti Earthquake
Religion, Natural Hazards and Disaster Response
Roger P. Abbott and Robert S. White

The Bible, Social Media and Digital Culture
Peter M. Phillips

Religious Studies and the Goal of Interdisciplinarity
Brent Smith

Visual Thought in Russian Religious Philosophy
Pavel Florensky's Theory of the Icon
Clemena Antonova

For more information about this series, please visit: www.routledge.com/Routledge-Focus-on-Religion/book-series/RFR

"This is the first important study that draws attention to the importance of the visual theme in Russian religious philosophy and its contemporary significance. In doing so, the author makes a highly original contribution to the field."
— **Rudolf Prokschi**, *Professor Emeritus, Department of Historical Theology, University of Vienna, Austria*

"This book is not just of interest to the relatively small circle of experts in Russian religious philosophy, but deserves a much wider readership. The monograph is well researched, lucid, and very accessible, but without oversimplifying the complexity of the material. Antonova convincingly argues that the intermediation between Christian theology, philosophy, and aesthetics, characteristic of Florensky's writings, was a response to the crisis of modernity and an attempt to evade the erosion of Christian metaphysics. Florensky's daring and creative engagement with Byzantine theology, Cubism, Non-Euclidean geometry, and set theory was motivated by the need for a consistently Christian vision of the world."
— **Christoph Schneider**, *Academic Director, Institute for Orthodox Christian Studies, Cambridge, UK*

"Florensky's religious philosophy has great relevance for understanding pictorial art. In particular, his theory of the icon comprehends the spectator-image relation in a way that challenges familiar Western notions of pictorial representation. Clemena Antonova's fine book throws much light on these issues, and presents Florensky's ideas in a sparkling way that illuminates their relevance for many other aspects of religious thought in the contemporary world."
— **Paul Crowther**, *Professor Emeritus in Philosophy, National University of Ireland, Galway, and member of the Royal Irish Academy*

"In this important book, Antonova offers a comprehensive analysis of what one may call the new theology of visuality of Pavel Florensky, which has influenced thinkers in Russia and beyond."
— **Alexei Lidov**, *Professor at Moscow State University, Russia, member of the Russian Academy of Arts, and member of St. Catherine's College, Oxford, UK*

Visual Thought in Russian Religious Philosophy
Pavel Florensky's Theory of the Icon

Clemena Antonova

LONDON AND NEW YORK

First published 2020 by Routledge

2 Park Square, Milton Park, Abingdon, Oxon, OX14 4RN

605 Third Avenue, New York, NY 10017

Routledge is an imprint of the Taylor & Francis Group, an informa business

First issued in paperback 2020

Copyright © 2020 Clemena Antonova

The right of Clemena Antonova to be identified as author of this work has been asserted by her in accordance with sections 77 and 78 of the Copyright, Designs and Patents Act 1988.

All rights reserved. No part of this book may be reprinted or reproduced or utilised in any form or by any electronic, mechanical, or other means, now known or hereafter invented, including photocopying and recording, or in any information storage or retrieval system, without permission in writing from the publishers.

Notice:
Product or corporate names may be trademarks or registered trademarks, and are used only for identification and explanation without intent to infringe.

British Library Cataloguing-in-Publication Data
A catalogue record for this book is available from the British Library

Library of Congress Cataloging-in-Publication Data
Names: Antonova, Clemena, 1970– author.
Title: Visual thought in Russian religious philosophy : Pavel Florensky's theory of the icon / Clemena Antonova.
Description: New York, New York : Routledge, 2019. | Series: Routledge focus on religion | Includes bibliographical references and index.
Identifiers: LCCN 2019029787 (print) | LCCN 2019029788 (ebook) | ISBN 9780367206826 (hardback) | ISBN 9780429262890 (ebook)
Subjects: LCSH: Florenskiĭ, P. A. (Pavel Aleksandrovich), 1882–1937. | Icons. | Philosophical theology. | Philosophy and religion—Russia. | Philosophy, Russian—20th century.
Classification: LCC BX597.F6 A68 2019 (print) | LCC BX597.F6 (ebook) | DDC 230/.19092—dc23
LC record available at https://lccn.loc.gov/2019029787
LC ebook record available at https://lccn.loc.gov/2019029788

ISBN: 978-0-367-20682-6 (hbk)
ISBN: 978-0-367-77783-8 (pbk)

Typeset in Times New Roman
by Apex CoVantage, LLC

Contents

List of figures viii
Acknowledgements ix

Introduction: Florensky's project of religious modernity   1

1 The unity of man and God before the icon: the icon as "energetic symbol"   22

2 The unity of the icon in space: on a stage in man's road to deification   36

3 The unity of faith and reason: on an unusual application of Non-Euclidean geometry   52

4 The organic unity of the icon and the Church ritual as a synthesis of the arts   66

Conclusion and implications   80

Bibliography 86
Index 97

Figures

2.1 Natalia Goncharova, *Portrait of Mikhail Larionov*, 1913, Museum Ludwig, Köln/Cologne, Schenkung Sammlung Ludwig/Donation Ludwig Collection 2011; permission by Rheinisches Bildarchiv, Cologne (RBA)   38

2.2 *St. Mark the Evangelist*, Russian, Tver School, sixteenth century, 55.5 × 41.5 cm., Temple Gallery, London; permission by the Temple Gallery and Richard Temple   39

2.3 *The Death of St. Nicholas*, Russian, Mstera School, late nineteenth century, 31.5 × 27.0 cm., Temple Gallery, London; permission by the Temple Gallery and Richard Temple   40

3.1 Geometry on a sphere, illustrating Riemann's variant of Non-Euclidean geometry; drawing and permission by Marian Kovacik   56

3.2 *Mary Receiving the Purple*, Kariye Camii, Constantinople, ca. 1304, inner narthex, bay 3, West, wall lunette; permission by Dumbarton Oaks   61

3.3 Reconstruction of the building to the viewer's left in Figure 3.2; my drawing   61

3.4 Barrel-like deformations: (a) Novgorod School, thirteenth century, fragment from an icon; (b) twelfth century, fragment from a miniature; (c) Italian, thirteenth century; fragment from an icon (from Zhegin, see bibliography)   62

4.1 Fresco by Costas Vafiadis. The image of late Russian leader Lenin (R) is painted on the wall of the Greek Orthodox church of the Holy Virgin in Axioupolis, northern Greece; Reuters/Griogoris Siamidis, 6 February 2007   67

Acknowledgements

There are a number of individuals and institutions whose contribution to the present book I would like to acknowledge.

Firstly, the general theoretical framework of the book grew out of my research for the "Religion and Secularism" programme directed by Charles Taylor, one of the most influential philosophers nowadays, at the Institute for Human Sciences in Vienna (IWM). This research was made possible by a two-year fellowship I was granted by the Austrian Science Fund. Most of the writing up took place at the IWM at a later stage in the context of my work for political scientist Ivan Krastev's programme, "Eurasia in Global Dialogue." Generally, the environment at the institute in Vienna was an important factor for the re-orientation of my work as an art historian towards the application of art-historical research to contemporary social and philosophical issues. This approach was also motivated by a much earlier stay, as a Mellon Fellow, at the Institute for Advanced Studies in the Humanities at Edinburgh, where I was part of a project on the Enlightenment and anti-Enlightenment. I still hold fond memories of the generosity and kindness of the late director, Susan Manning.

Secondly, my art historical research was generously supported by fellowships I held at IMERA, the institute for advanced studies at the University of Aix-Provence, the MORPHOMATA Centre at the University of Cologne, and VLAC, the Centre at the Royal Academy of Belgium. If intelligent company in beautiful surroundings is anything to go by, at all these places I received the greatest support one could get. My research was also facilitated by my stays in Oxford every summer, where I have been teaching for the St. Bonaventure University programme at Trinity College. I thank the St. Bonaventure students and the Director of the programme, Michael Jones-Kelley, for making my time in England so enjoyable. Being in Oxford gave me access to an excellent library, but also provided me with the opportunity to discuss emerging ideas with my former D.Phil. supervisor, Martin Kemp, in his wonderful garden in Woodstock.

x *Acknowledgements*

Thirdly, the journal *Sobornost*, edited by Father Andrew Louth, one of foremost authorities in the field of Eastern Orthodox thought, has been very special to me. The following are some of the articles I published with *Sobornost*, which were expertly edited and commented on by Father Andrew and which became the foundation of parts of this book: " 'Daring to think' of a Non-Euclidean World: Science and Religion in Russian Critiques of the Icon" (2018), which received an essay prize from the Templeton Foundation; "How to View Icons: An Orthodox Theological View" (2015); and "Neo-Palamism in the Russian Philosophy of Full Unity: The Icon as Energetic Symbol" (2013). I also learned a lot from the anonymous reviewers of my two articles in the well-known journal *Leonardo*: "Non-Euclidean Geometry in the Russian History of Art: On a Little-known Application of a Scientific Theory" (2019) and "On the Problem of 'Reverse Perspective': Definitions East and West" (2010). I would further like to express my gratitude to the anonymous author of a highly challenging and deeply thought-provoking review of my chapter, "*Vseedinstvo*: A Russian Project of Religious Modernity and Its Contemporary Relevance" in the forthcoming volume, *Russia, Religion, and Secularism*, edited by Ana Siljak. Finally, Caryl Emerson wrote useful comments on my chapter titled "The Icon and the Visual Arts at the Time of the Russian Religious Renaissance," which is forthcoming in the *Oxford Handbook of Russian Religious Thought*. All these people have made me realize once again the value of receiving constructive criticism.

As numerous other academics from my country, Bulgaria, I received support from the Open Society Foundation, for which I feel sincerely grateful. I was also fortunate to have Jack Boothroyd from Routledge as the editor of the book.

My mother, Maria, read various versions of the manuscript and, as always, offered interesting and highly critical insights. My partner, Marian Kovacik, and my friends, Dessy Gavrilova and Biliana Hristova, deserve special thanks for their constant support all along. Without them, writing this book would not have been as pleasurable and easy-going as it proved to be, since, very simply, I would not have been able to concentrate on writing the book in the way I did. I can only wish that reading the book might give some pleasure to those who love Russian culture and those who value the experience provided by icons.

Clemena Antonova,
April 2019, Institute for Human Sciences, Vienna

Introduction
Florensky's project of religious modernity

Our contemporary modernity can be characterized by two overlapping developments: the so-called religious turn[1] and what has been termed the "pictorial turn."[2] In other words, religion has become increasingly prominent (in philosophy, in politics, in personal experiences, etc.), while, at the same time, modern culture has become highly visual to a degree and in a way never experienced before. These two dimensions of modern experience, while contemporaneous, are usually kept apart and studied in isolation. The present book brings the two themes of religion and visuality together by considering the work of one of the most intellectually exciting figures in Russian religious philosophy, Pavel Florensky (1882–1937). The material that the book covers will focus on Florensky's religious philosophy as conceptualized in his theory of the icon.

Firstly, it is suggested that while Florensky belongs to the Russian religious-philosophical movement of full unity (*vseedinstvo*), he stands out from this tradition in his profound engagement with visuality. While scholars – especially in Russia, less so in the West – have realized that full unity plays a significant role in Florensky's thought (see the following section on full unity), the originality of Florensky's approach, which is wedded to questions of visuality in terms of themes and concepts, has not yet been fully appreciated. One of the theses of this book is that Florensky's religious philosophy – which is so frequently, though not always, conceptualized through visual categories – is the Russian author's most original contribution to modern religious thought. What the Russian author does within the Orthodox tradition of the theology of the image is to re-energize the medieval, religious icon within the context of modern culture and the crisis of modernity. The very model of visuality that the sacred image presupposes is interpreted as an alternative to the reigning Western epistemological model of Kantian rationalism and Albertian perspectivism. For example, the spectatorial distance between viewing subject and passive object in Western philosophy, based on a rupture between subject and object, is completely changed. The presence contained within the symbolic image, the notion that the image stares back[3] suggests a fundamentally different relationship between the two, even a unity of sorts between subject and object.

Secondly, within the history of the problem of totality/unity/wholeness in European thought, the Russian religious-philosophical interpretation is very little known. At the same time, the Russian preoccupation with the concept of full unity, grounded as it is in a modern, religious worldview, can offer valuable insights in the context of present-day discussions of the relationship between secular and religious reason and the role of religion in modernity. While I believe that full unity is not as uniquely Russian, as its representatives and their followers like to present it, I will suggest that Florensky's brand of it – a rethinking of Orthodox theological ideas framed against a preoccupation with the visual theme – is highly original. Moreover, I argue that Florensky's approach comes the closest to providing a working model of the Russian ideal of full unity. Florensky puts the medieval image forward as a visual model of unity. While playing on traditional Orthodox themes, he expresses them in a modern idiom with modern concerns in view.

In my reading, Florensky's project can be described as one of "religious modernity."[4] This may sound surprising to those who have accepted the predominant, but unexamined, view that Russian religious thought is, almost by definition, traditionalist, exclusively backward-looking, mystical, and anti-rationalist. There are, no doubt, such trends and they are not exclusive to the Russian case – there is a strong mystical tradition in Western theology, while the stand against rationalism and positivism has been a feature of much of Western philosophy throughout the twentieth century. What makes Russian religious philosophy specific is the brand of "religious modernity" it offers – an Orthodox, Christian religiosity which embraces naturally, and even presupposes, characteristics which are commonly seen as aspects of secularity. In this way, it questions the much debated recently concept of secularism.[5]

The period at the end of the nineteenth and the beginning of the twentieth centuries, frequently referred to as the Russian Silver Age, was one of the most vibrant and exciting moments in the intellectual history of the twentieth century. Avant-garde experiments in painting, the cinema, the theatre, and music put Russia in the forefront of the emergence of modernism. Developments in mathematics placed the Russians on the map of scientists worldwide. Symbolism, the revival of occultism and of Platonic idealism, and the renewed interest in German romantic philosophy and in Nietzsche further enriched the intellectual landscape. What underlies all these seemingly disparate developments, though, is the idea that religion and modernity belong together. In many ways and under different forms, there was a fusion of a revived Orthodoxy and a modernism that we tend to think of as exclusively secular. It is noteworthy that the religious philosophy of the *vseedintsy* (the representatives of full unity, or *vseedinstvo*) frequently ran counter to the positions of the Russian Orthodox Church. In fact, almost all the representatives of the movement had a tense or at least an ambiguous relationship with the official Church, including Soloviev and Bulgakov (Bulgakov was almost excommunicated in the 1930s by the Russian Church Abroad). Florensky himself became known for his vocal support of teachings that the Russian Church had declared heretical in no uncertain terms (for instance, his defence of the Name-Worshippers, discussed in Chapter 1). In other words, it cannot be emphasized enough that the most exciting ideas during what was called "the Russian religious renaissance"[6] at the beginning of the twentieth century were formulated almost entirely outside the channels provided by the Church and frequently were violently opposed by the Church hierarchy.

Florensky's writings – which, as we will see, make contact with all the major trends of the Silver Age – demonstrate this fusion to an extreme degree. One could describe Florensky's method as a constant process of "Christianizing" and "Orthodoxizing" of the contemporary material (from art history, mathematics, physics, etc.) that he was working with.

Intellectual biography: a note

For my purposes, a short note outlining the main stages of Pavel Florensky's (1882–1937) intellectual evolution is sufficient.[7] For a standard biography of Florensky, the reader is referred to Avril Pyman's recent *Pavel Florensky: A Quiet Genius* (2010),[8] which is the first book of the kind in English, and an excellently documented and balanced account of a complex personality.

Florensky grew up in a cultured and completely irreligious family, a factor which explains, at least in part, the strong sense of a personal journey towards God in his religious philosophy. He experienced a spiritual crisis during his last year at school in Tiflis, Georgia, which led him to Christianity. During his studies at the Physico-Mathematical Faculty at Moscow University (1900–1904), he became closely involved with the world-famous Moscow School of Mathematics. At the same time, he was attending the philosophy seminars of the prominent Russian thinkers Lev Lopatin and Sergei Trubetskoy at the Historical-Philosophical Faculty. Working and thinking at the crossroads of disciplines became a permanent characteristic of his intellectual make-up henceforth. A degree in theology at the Moscow Theological Academy followed (1904–1908) and then priesthood (1911). Florensky's Master's thesis at the Academy, when published as *Stolp i utverzhdenie istini* (The Pillar and Ground of the Truth) (1914, revised edition), became hugely influential. The book is generally regarded as a theological treatise, but it can be also described as a personal account of a modern person's discovery of God. Very appropriately, it is written in the form of twelve letters to a friend, on topics such as the theological dogma of the Trinity, the conception of Sophia, etc. While the subjects sound familiar, the author's treatment of them is highly unconventional. A mathematical problem by Lewis Carroll, the Oxford mathematician and author of *Alice in Wonderland*, provides a helping hand in the discussion of the dogma of Trinity.[9] The paradox of the Trinity is set alongside the problem of irrationality in modern mathematics. The icon of the Annunciation with its symbolic colours is discussed in the context of the Sophia concept.

Florensky's book *Smisl' idealizma* (The Meaning of Idealism) came out in the same year as the *Pillar*, and at the time and since it has been largely overshadowed by the latter. It is an important work, though, as it casts light on some of the affiliations of the author that characterize all his work: a commitment to an idealist position in the sense of Platonic idealism, a tendency to closely ally Christianity with its Platonic genealogy, and an interest in questions of visuality and specially the organization of pictorial space and concerns shared with modernism and the European and Russian avant-garde. The book, which is available only in Russian at this stage, is one of the main points of reference in Chapter 2.

In the aftermath of the October Revolution (1917), Florensky worked for the Soviets in the field of applied science and held a number of high-ranking positions, including at the State Commission for Electrification. There are a dozen patents in his name for scientific and technological inventions from this period. One gets the impression that the transition to more practically oriented and scientifically focused positions must have been smooth, as Florensky never found a conflict between science, religion, and philosophy. Thus, the chief editor of *Bogoslovskii vestnik* (Theological Journal) from 1911 to 1917 became the editor of *Tekhnologicheskaia entsiklopediia* (Technological Encyclopaedia) from 1927 onwards. Florensky's writings on art, which would later attract the attention of semioticians and art historians (for example, the classic essay "Reverse Perspective" written in 1919) also belong to the early years of Soviet rule. Particularly in the first half of the 1920s, while teaching at VKhUTEMAS (the Higher Art-technical Studios, later the Higher Artistic and Technical Institute) and RAKhN (the Russian Academy of Artistic Sciences, later the State Academy of Artistic Sciences), a lot of the work he did related to visuality and especially pictorial space. At RAKhN, he described himself in his autobiography as a "professor in the analysis of space."[10]

Florensky always believed that the antinomy between knowledge and faith was illusory, as both were "equally necessary for man, equally valuable and sacred."[11] Probably for this very reason, he never saw the need to downplay his religious associations. The photographs of Florensky, clad in his priestly cassock at various engineering and other scientific conferences, remain memorable. It is possible that his arrest, first in 1927 and then in 1933, ending with his execution in 1937, was part of the purges of not only religiously minded intellectuals, priests, and philosophers, but also scientists.[12]

"I capture every thought to make it obedient to Christ:" the Russian concept of full unity

Modern studies on Florensky invariably draw attention to the huge scope of the Russian writer's expertise in diverse fields of knowledge and the interdisciplinary nature of his writings. The frequent references to Florensky as "the Russian Leonardo" are, generally, meant exactly in this sense.[13] Every now and again a new aspect of his work is uncovered: he wrote religious philosophy, but also worked on electricity and was interested in magic; he invented a machine oil that the Soviets used for several decades, but also wrote Symbolist poetry, etc. All this is true. What becomes somewhat obscured in this presentation is that Florensky's approach is not just a matter of personal ability and subjective preference, but it belongs to a whole line of thought within Russian religious philosophy going back to the nineteenth century with the Slavophile philosophers and especially Vladimir Soloviev (1853–1900).

The view that a very particular movement within Russian religious philosophy can be identified and that it can be defined by the adherence of its followers to the concept of *vseedinstvo* has been vigorously promoted by some Russian authors. The English translation of *vseedinstvo* has included "total unity,"[14] "pan-unity,"[15] and "spiritual unity."[16] My own preference for "full unity," the term I will use henceforth, is dictated by a concern to avoid the association with pantheism (of "pan-unity"), with totalitarianism in politics (in "total unity"), and with the value-laden opposition between the spiritual and the material (in "spiritual unity").[17] V.N. Akulinin, in a study titled *The Philosophy of Full Unity: From V.S. Soloviev to P.A. Florensky* (1990, in Russian) claims that there is "a philosophical school of full unity"[18] which is "distinguishable from other schools and philosophical trends in Russia."[19] This school, founded by Soloviev, is based on the "originality of the conception of full unity."[20] Its main representatives, whom Akulinin calls "*vseedintsy*," are the brothers Sergei and Evgeny Trubetskoy, Sergei Bulgakov, V. F. Ern, etc., while Florensky represents the culmination and the last stage of the movement. Earlier, in *The Russian Idea* (1946), Nikolay Berdyaev, probably the best-known Russian philosopher in the West, had also proposed that the "totalitarian character" (from

6   Introduction

"total unity") of thought constitutes a "peculiar originality" of Russian religious philosophy.[21] In a well-known work, *A History of Russian Philosophy* (1948) another Russian émigré, Vasilii Zenkovsky, also mentions a line of philosophizing which he describes as the "metaphysics of total-unity."[22]

If we accept that there is a philosophical movement or even school of "full unity" within the Russian tradition, then even a cursory glance reveals that the concept of full unity was used to cover a wide range of phenomena – it was applied to human consciousness, to the world as a whole, to the relationship between the subject and object in the process of knowledge, to the relationship between the imminent and the transcendent, to the notion of a universal Church, etc. All these connotations are inter-connected and represent facets of the underlying connectedness of Being. This book will refer to several meanings of full unity, which lay in the background of Florensky's critique of the icon. On the one hand, the experience of the viewer before the icon opens the possibility for the unity between God and man (Chapter 1). On the other, there is the unity of the image itself, brought about by the organization of the pictorial space of the icon (Chapter 2). Further, the very critique of the icon as a visual model of Non-Euclidean geometry is a demonstration of the unity of faith and reason (Chapter 3). Finally, the holy icon exists in a unity with the holy space of the Church and the church ritual (Chapter 4).

The idea that knowledge is one and that it is revealed to the whole man, who exercises all his powers of cognition (rationality, mystical intuition, aesthetic perception, etc.), an idea mostly familiar from Soloviev,[23] was very important for the earlier, so-called Slavophile philosophers, Aleksei Khomiakov (1804–1860) and Ivan Kireevsky (1806–1856). The Slavophiles wrote about the "inner wholeness of self-consciousness"[24] and condemned Western thought for separating reason from "its original unity with the other faculties of the human spirit."[25] They called for an "inner wholeness of the mind for the comprehension of integral truth" through a "coordination of all cognitive powers into a single force."[26] Soloviev, who was the direct intellectual descendant of the Slavophiles, never tired of emphasizing the need for an "organic synthesis of theology, philosophy, and the experimental sciences." "Only such a synthesis," in his view, "can comprise the whole truth of knowledge."[27]

The discussion of full unity and, by implication, of integral knowledge, from Khomiakov and Kireevsky, through Soloviev and to Florensky, was invariably couched in terms of the opposition between the alleged fragmentariness of Western philosophy and the full unity that Russian religious philosophy had set itself as its task. There is some irony in this position, having in mind that the immediate roots of the concept of full unity lie in Western thought,[28] especially German romantic philosophy (the term in

German is *All-Einheit*).[29] Hegel's philosophy, much of which can be read as an elaboration of his slogan "the true is the whole,"[30] was important, though not always acknowledged. The German *All-Einheit* resonated among nineteenth-century theologians such as Jakob Sengler, who in his *Der Idee Gottes* (1845) interpreted the term as a pantheistic, anti-Christian concept. In Russia, though, no one had an influence comparable to that of Schelling. The powerful evocation of aesthetic unity/wholeness with Schelling, and his notion of art as "theurgy" (i.e. the ability of art to embody transcendental form), made him indispensable to Florensky's own project. Ultimately, the origins of full unity go back at least to Plato[31] and the Neo-Platonists.[32] From the Fathers of the Church to mystical teaching in the Middle Ages, full unity took a new life. The Platonic and Christian underpinnings, which are fundamental for understanding Florensky's *oeuvre*, always hover in the background of Russian religious philosophy. What comes probably more as a surprise is the recourse of religious philosophers in Russia to Spinoza's attempt, within a worldview that denied a Judaeo-Christian God, to conceptualize full unity.[33] Martin Jay has even suggested that the concept of "totality" arises in modern times in the Enlightenment and is especially evident in the confidence in the capacity of mankind to know the world.[34]

Thus, the Russian religious-philosophical concept of full unity illustrates once again the futility of attempting to draw a clear-cut opposition between Russia and the West. As we saw, the Russians themselves – the representatives of full unity, as well as Russian scholars, mostly emigrés to the West, who have been promoting the movement abroad – have passionately insisted on the uniqueness and originality of full unity. Their motivation largely grows from the inherited Slavophile tradition, first articulated in the 1820s, of viewing Russia and the Russian people (*narod*) as having a special role to play in world history. These early nineteenth-century ideas of national purpose cast a shadow over the Silver Age as well and provided the background against which the opposition between Russia and the West was formulated. In the case of full unity, the heritage that the Russians built on was, as can be noticed from the brief overview above in this chapter, mostly, though not completely, Western, largely pagan or at least outside mainstream Christianity, when not openly anti-religious. What Russian religious philosophers attempted to do – sometimes successfully, sometimes not – was to take the concept of full unity and thoroughly Christianize it and "Orthodoxize" it, while keeping and further developing the modern idiom. As Soloviev wrote in a letter of 1873:

> It is now clear to me as two times two is four that the whole great development of Western philosophy and science, apparently indifferent and

often hostile to Christianity, has in fact merely elaborated for Christianity a new form – one that is worthy of it.[35]

Probably no one had a better right that Florensky, who was deeply immersed in Western philosophy and science and was at the same time whole-heartedly committed to an Orthodox Christian worldview, to say along with St. Paul, "I capture every thought to make it obedient to Christ" (2 Corinthians).

Indeed, for Florensky and for the whole Russian tradition, it is faith that is "the pillar and the ground of truth."[36] It is, therefore, important to realize that all studies on art, philosophy, mathematics, etc. by representatives of the school of full unity, are grounded in a profoundly felt and thought-through Christian worldview. Even more significantly, it can be maintained that what holds these different aspects of knowledge together (i.e. what makes knowledge "integral" and unified) is faith. Florensky's call that "we should philosophize *in* religion"[37] and his view that philosophy is "valuable not in itself [. . .] but for the life in Christ"[38] applies to all fields of intellectual investigation.

Thus, to describe the Russian philosophical enterprise in general and Florensky's in particular as an interdisciplinary exercise can be very misleading, so long as we understand interdisciplinarity as insights from different disciplines which, brought together, could illuminate a certain problem in frequently unexpected and intellectually exciting ways. An interdisciplinary approach in this sense is, no doubt, a worthy intellectual endeavour. However, it seems to me that it is very different from the belief, which is religious in nature, that it is the duty of man to strive to know the Truth, and the only way to do so is by bringing together the scattered facets of the one Truth. We may call this approach interdisciplinary, but we should not lose sight of its profound religious and moral implications.

In the case of Florensky, whatever evolution is notable with respect to some of his ideas, what remains remarkably consistent from his student days to the end of his life is the commitment to the project of full unity, understood especially in the sense of the unity of secular and religious reason. In a letter of 3 March 1904 to his mother, he wrote of his intention to "conduct a synthesis of ecclesiastical and profane culture, to integrate with the church, but without compromise and with honesty, to apprehend the positive doctrine of the church, the scientific and philosophical worldviews, and so on."[39] In 1937, the year of his death, in one of his last letters from prison, addressed to his son Kiril, he looks back at his work and says:

> I investigated the world as a whole, as one picture and one reality. More precisely, at each given moment or at each step of my life I made this investigation and from a particular angle of vision. I would investigate

the relationship of the world by dissecting it in a particular direction, on a particular plane, and would strive to understand the make-up of the world from the plane that interested me. Each plane was different, but the one did not contradict the next. The one simply enriched the other. This resulted in perpetual dialectic of thought, an exchange of planes of observation, while at the same time the world was still being viewed as one.[40]

This extract merits a full quotation, as it refers to the idea of full unity which cuts across Florensky's work and connects it with basically all the intellectual currents in the Silver Age. The Wagnerian notion of the synthesis of the arts, which was embraced by Vasilii Kandinsky and others of the avant-garde, is seen by Florensky as operative in religious ritual (Chapter 4), while the metaphor of Non-Euclidean geometry, circulating among avant-garde poets and artists, is in the background of Florensky's theory of pictorial space in the icon (see Chapter 3).

In many ways, the Russian project of full unity ultimately failed as it could not produce a convincing philosophical explanation of the world that would decisively supplant the Western Enlightenment and post-Enlightenment, framework. It proved too vague, too utopian, and it was riddled with various philosophical and theological problems. The main contribution of the philosophy of full unity, in my reading, was to further open Christian thought to modernity. Philosophers such as Soloviev and Bulgakov may not have come out with the solutions to the problems of modernity, but they attracted attention, to an unprecedented extent, to questions which are still relevant and urgent, especially to those concerned with the role of religion in the modern world. At the same time, I believe that it was Florensky, in his work on the icon, who came closest to providing a working and coherent model of the Russian project.

The Eastern Orthodox icon, in Florensky's interpretation, becomes a concrete, visual model of the theoretical concept of full unity. I argue that the value of Florensky's approach lies exactly in bringing together themes at the crossroads of visuality, religion, and modernity. The task I have set myself in this book is to reconstruct Florensky's theory of the image from his scattered, frequently fragmentary, and often unfinished writings, and to set it in the context of the Russian writer's religious-philosophical position, which he shares with the school of full unity.

"Seeing the soul embodied": the icon as concrete metaphysics

In the 1930s, while in prison, Florensky wrote a poem titled "Oro."[41] The poem is about the boy Oro, who is from a Siberian tribe and is the hope for salvation of his people. We know that Oro is special, in part, because of his ability to think through images rather than through concepts. In other words, Oro is like the ancient Egyptian sages that Plotinus talks about, who thought in images, the original mode of human thought (*Enneads*, V.II).[42] Oro is emblematic of a concern that Florensky had had throughout his creative life: i.e. to put the image, particularly the Eastern Orthodox icon, forward as the model of what he called a "concrete metaphysics of being."[43] Images, of course, are not exclusively visual – there are mental, verbal images, etc. At the same time, visuality does play a very special role in the Russian author's project. The concern with visuality was so dear to Florensky's heart that he felt he had to emphasize it in a highly intimate text, his testament to his children, in which he wrote that all his life he had "wanted *to see* the soul," but he had wanted "*to see it embodied*."[44] As was already mentioned, it is this profound engagement with visuality that, I believe, constitutes Florensky's most valuable contribution to Russian religious philosophy. It is also his most powerful bid to participate in present-day discussions that take place at the crossroads between a "pictorial turn" and a "religious turn" in modern culture.

One cannot help noticing Florensky's almost obsessive concern with the medieval Russian icon. Indeed, art historians, especially those interested in medieval art and questions of pictorial space, have become increasingly fascinated by Florensky's works on the sacred image since the publication in 1967, for the first time, of his essay "Reverse Perspective."[45] My initial interest in Florensky largely focused on the same art-history-related material.[46] It is both useful and rewarding to look into the Russian writer's texts on the medieval icon. At the same time, and in view of what was mentioned in the previous section, it would be misleading to create the impression that Florensky was an "art historian" in the narrow sense of the word.[47] It is true that Florensky deals with questions which are part of the standard repertoire of art history, most famously pictorial space and the so-called reverse perspective. Still, I believe that no one would have been more surprised than Florensky himself if he realized that he was being labelled as an "art historian" in the conventional sense of the word. There is no visual analysis for its own sake with Florensky, nor is there a history of art narrowly conceived. The icon is of enormous importance to Florensky not as representing a stage in the evolution of art, but as a concrete, visual model of a profoundly thought-through religious-philosophical position, growing out of the Russian tradition of full unity. The sacred image is the unity of this and the other world, it is the meeting ground between God and man, where God acts through His energies that are accessible to man and discloses His presence to man. It is in this sense that the icon is defined as symbol (see Chapter 1). All these ideas are familiar from the age-old Eastern

Orthodox tradition on the theology of the image, but it was Florensky who re-interpreted them in the framework of the interests and concerns, even the anxieties, of modern man.

The interest in issues of aesthetics and, in some cases, in the icon in particular, keeps lurking in the background of the Russian philosophy of full unity. Already Soloviev had planned to write a study on aesthetics, though he never came to doing it. One of his followers, Evgeny Trubetskoy, wrote three pieces on the Russian icon between 1914 and 1917, which proved highly influential.[48] Sergei Bulgakov, another member of the philosophical school of full unity, was also interested in the problem of the religious image.[49] This makes sense in view of the main orientation of the philosophy of full unity. A careful reading shows that the rhetoric of Russian writers is always addressed not against reason as such but against the *abstract* and *passive* logical reason of much of Western thought. Hence there comes the commitment to *living* religious experience and the *concrete* appearance of thought, notions repeated over and over again by all the philosophers of full unity. With Florensky this idea is especially pronounced. As the contemporary Russian philosopher Sergei Khoruzii has noted in several works, "concreteness" (*konkretnost'*) is the main characteristic principle of Florensky's metaphysics."[50] In an autobiographical note, Florensky says of himself: "By denying the abstraction of logical thought, Florensky sees the value of thought in its concrete appearance (*konkretnom iavlenii*)."[51] "Concreteness" as opposed to abstract reason finds an expression in many ways but nowhere as decisively as in the visual image, because for Florensky "the spiritual object" is always "concrete, visible."[52]

The focus on the icon and the concept of "concrete metaphysics" belong to a tradition in Eastern Orthodoxy which stresses the value of the material. Thus, a thing, an object such as the religious icon, is believed to be able to embody the spiritual and the transcendent. As St. John of Damascus, one of the major Iconophile writers in the eighth century, claimed: "I honour [matter] not as God, but as something filled with divine energy and grace."[53] In the same vein, at the end of the nineteenth and the beginning of the twentieth century, Russian thinkers such as Soloviev and Bulgakov would use the term "religious materialism" to describe their philosophical position. The idea of the value of the material underlines the Eastern Orthodox theology of the image and makes possible the tradition of thought on the "theology of the icon."

Recently, there have been some thought-provoking studies by philosophers and scholars in visual studies which have addressed the religious and metaphysical significance of pictorial art.[54] There has also been a revived interest, especially among scholars of religion, in the so-called theology through the arts: i.e. the possibility that the arts (music, architecture,

12 Introduction

iconography, etc.) could "inculcate theological ideas without, however, providing ultimate theological paradigms."[55] In German scholarship there is a line of thought that goes back to the nineteenth century which considers ways in which Gothic architecture may be seen as expressing notions and doctrines that were developed by the Scholastic theology of the day. The most famous example is Erwin Panofsky's *Gothic Architecture and Scholasticism* (1951).[56] Already in the nineteenth century, Ferdinand Piper had coined the term "monumental theology,"[57] which is based on the notion that artistic monuments are as important for the study of theology as the texts themselves.[58] However, it is attempts at a "theology through images," understood exactly as visual images, that have proved the most sensitive topics, as the various iconoclastic movements within the Church manifest. The dramatic history of iconoclasm is very much the result of the belief that theological ideas can be "carried not only by the text but by the image in the icon itself."[59] Charles Barber[60] and other scholars (including myself)[61] have considered the topic of "theology through images" specifically in a Byzantine and an Eastern Orthodox context. As Robin Cormack notes, in Byzantium "icons were accepted as a mode through which one reaches closer to an explanation of God than any verbal definition could ever do."[62] The possibility of "theology through images" and more generally of "visual thought," however, is both promising and problematic, so long as we are dealing with mental processes that have to do with the conceptual and logical, on the one hand, and the non-conceptual and intuitive, on the other.[63] In this work, I am approaching Florensky's writings on the icon as a case study in "visual thought" (i.e. the icon is interpreted along lines that disclose profound, philosophical ideas). Doing religious philosophy through the consistent employment of visual, alongside philosophical and theological, categories, is, I believe, what makes Florensky attractive to the modern reader.

Florensky today: a Christianity gone worldly

What is the significance of Russian religious philosophy in general and Florensky in particular, if any, in today's world? Can Florensky's work from the beginning of the twentieth century be relevant again at the beginning of the twenty-first century? I am proposing in this book that Florensky's approach to the Russian concept of full unity in his theory of the icon can contribute in interesting and important ways to ongoing discussions on the interrelationship between religion, modernity, and art.

Modernity is frequently understood as defined by the "death of God" (Nietzsche) and by "disenchantment" (Weber). It is allegedly profoundly secular. This is certainly true in the sense that we no longer live in the unquestioningly religious world of older times. It is, however, as glaringly obvious that religion, in one form or another, remains important to millions of people around the world. Actually, if anything, religious longing and spiritual quest have become even more prominent in the last several decades. Some authors have suggested that we live in "a new age of religious searching, whose outcome no one can foresee."[64] Not only on the level of the individual, but on the level of society at large, religion has taken a new, public role. José Casanova has written about the "deprivatization" of religion since the 1980s: i.e. the fact that "religious traditions around the world are refusing to accept the marginal and privatized role which theories of modernity and theories of secularization had reserved for them."[65] As a result, if religion could be described as "invisible"[66] (i.e. existing on the margins of culture), a couple of decades earlier, more recently it has become clearly noticeable that religion has entered the public sphere.

These new developments, however, are connected to a re-framing of what constitutes religion and religious experience. The transformation goes back to "the change in religious consciousness since the Reformation and the Enlightenment,"[67] but it has become particularly noticeable in the last half century. Charles Taylor has convincingly argued that especially the last fifty years can be characterized by a *"change in the conditions of belief."*[68] Religious belief has become open to doubt and critique as never before. The coming of the secular age, in Taylor's view, is marked by a "titanic change in Western civilization,"[69] which reveals itself in the transformation "from a society in which it was virtually impossible not to believe in God to one in which faith, even to the staunchest believer, is one human possibility among many."[70] This change was remarked already in the late 1960s by scholars such as Peter Berger.[71]

Some scholars, including those in conservative and traditionalist circles within the Catholic and Orthodox Churches, lament the self-reflective, questioning attitude to Christianity and have, at times, opposed it in no uncertain terms. One cannot deny that this new religiosity can contribute to the anxiety of the modern condition. It goes hand in hand with the typically modern sense of a loss of meaning and of a painful absence often understood, from Hölderlin to Heidegger and many others, as a religious absence, the fear that "if men had forgotten what it means to exist religiously, they had doubtless also forgotten what it means to exist as human beings."[72] Others, like Nietzsche, have celebrated man's ability and courage to face the void.[73] There are, however, also those who feel the need for God and want to open Christianity to modernity, approaching religion as living experience, as constant quest, and as enhancing man's full potential. Members of this group, who subscribe to what the theologian Paul Tillich called a "larger concept of religion,"[74] can be described as the "religious seekers";

to them, Russian religious philosophy and Florensky in particular cannot fail to be of interest.

It is within a wider understanding of religion, which, according to Fr. Vladimir (Fedorov), a professor at the Theological Academy in St. Petersburg, regards the mission of the Church as "the uncovering of the whole creative potential of man," that Florensky has a role to play.[75] In many ways, Florensky represents a "Christianity that has gone worldly."[76] This position is not without its risks, as we can see from the extreme and passionate reactions (both positive and negative) that Florensky's works have produced. Georges Florovsky, one of the foremost Russian émigré theologians, for instance, has accused Florensky of being a "stranger to the Orthodox world."[77] Florensky himself never tired of insisting on his Orthodoxy and his belonging to the Church. From a strictly confessional and dogmatic point of view, however, his position has been seen as "pouring new wine into old bottles," while trying "to show that the old bottles had been waiting for just that wine."[78] I suggest that it is exactly this very specific fusion between tradition and modernity, of "old bottles" and "new wine" that makes Florensky appealing. In my reading, this fusion constitutes a thoroughgoing Christian worldview in the wider sense of modern Christianity. The dozens and dozens of accounts by Florensky's contemporaries, who have claimed that the Russian thinker "furthered [their] return to the Church,"[79] point to the possibilities that Florensky's philosophy could open up.

It seems to me that it is clear that there is no way back to a pre-Enlightenment and pre-Reformation Christianity, no matter whether we consider this a good or a bad thing. What is remarkable, however, is that it is becoming increasingly obvious that we cannot stick, just as unreflectively, to a worldview that radically excludes the transcendental dimension from human existence. In *Religion in the Contemporary World*, Steve Bruce observes that "the fragmentation of religious culture was, in time, to see the widespread, taken-for-granted, and unexamined Christianity of the pre-Reformation period replaced by an equally widespread, taken-for-granted, and unexamined indifference to religion."[80] It is this "taken-for-granted" and "unexamined indifference to religion" that is, I believe, for some at least, no longer viable in a globalized world in which religion, sometimes in dramatic ways, shows itself increasingly capable of determining many people's identities, allegiances, and worldviews. One of the characteristic features of present-day culture is that there is no clear-cut distinction between believers and non-believers, despite the perception of some on each side. There is a growing group of people who may not describe themselves as believers but still ask themselves religious questions and live in "a state of ultimate concern about something ultimate."[81]

The "turn to religion" in recent philosophy – in continental philosophy and also in the analytical tradition[82] – has been growing stronger. As Habermas mentioned during his 2004 dialogue with Ratzinger (cardinal at the time, later Pope Benedict XVI), what can be noticed is philosophy's "self-reflection with regard to its own religious-metaphysical origins."[83] We see more and more a willingness to critique a narrow secularism and the implied secular–religious divide by authors who are committed Christians (Charles Taylor), but also by those are not (Habermas). Thus, there have been calls for a "critical overcoming of [. . .] a narrow secular consciousness,"[84] which are reflected in such increasingly popular terms as "post-secularism" and "post-secular philosophy."[85]

In the process, "post-secular philosophy" touches on problems and issues that are at the heart of the Russian project. The Russian intellectual tradition with which I am concerned was founded on the conscious rejection of the Western opposition between religion and secularism, a problem which is addressed by a number of modern thinkers.[86] Its ultimate aim was to work out an alternative epistemological model which would realize the ideal of full unity. While the Russians may have failed in producing such a model, their profound engagement with the problem of full unity in a religious context draws a bridge to work done in the West at the time and later. Jacques Maritain, for instance, reveals often strikingly similar concerns (and even language) in some of his writings, such as *Integral Humanism* (1936). An intellectually significant, but little known, development is the impact of Russian religious philosophy, mainly via the émigré thinkers in Paris and through French publications, on the Second Vatican Council (1962–1965).[87] The Council represented a rare and important endeavour on part of the Catholic Church to open Christianity to modernity. Recent studies draw attention, over and over again, to the quest for unity and integrity of the individual in various forms of spiritual experiences,[88] while what are sometimes called "communitarian" philosophers such as Alasdair MacIntyre, Charles Taylor, Michael Walzer, Michael Sandel, etc. stress the importance of the community as a whole versus the exclusive value of individualism.[89]

Outline of chapters

The two organizing themes of full unity and visuality intersect, in various ways, throughout the material covered by this book.

Chapter 1, "The unity of man and God before the icon: the icon as 'energetic symbol'," looks at Florensky's definition of the icon as an "energetic symbol," which relies on drawing the visual implications of the teaching of the fourteenth-century Byzantine theologian St. Gregory Palamas. The Russian author appropriates the Palamite distinction between divine essence and energies, meant to describe the relationship between man and God, to describe the meaning of the icon as a "container" of the presence of God and, therefore, as a symbol (in a specific sense of the term), bringing about the unity of man and God, the immanent and the transcendent.

Chapter 2, "The unity of the icon in space: on a stage in man's road to deification," offers a theological reading of Florensky's theory of the pictorial space of the icon. It suggests that Florensky's notion of the "supplementary planes" of the icon in his classic essay "Reverse Perspective" (1919) was directly inspired by his earlier interest in Cubism, which he analyzed in his *The Meaning of Idealism* (1914). Both Cubist space and the spatial construction of the icon were interpreted as offering alternatives to Albertian perspectivism and Cartesian epistemology. The idea of "supplementary planes" is, in my view, useful because it can be interpreted as a stage in man's road to deification (*theosis*), a doctrine which is central in Eastern Orthodox Christianity and in Russian religious philosophy.

Chapter 3, "The unity of faith and reason: on an unusual application of Non-Euclidean geometry," considers again the problem of pictorial space with Florensky, but this time it draws attention to the Russian writer's little-known idea of space in the icon as Non-Euclidean. I suggest that Non-Euclidean geometry was a common theme in Russian intellectual history, going back especially to Dostoevsky. Florensky uses it in an unusual context: in his theory of the icon in view, once again, of attacking Renaissance perspective and the Kantian worldview. Moreover, by applying a fashionable scientific theory to questions of visuality and religion, he demonstrated his conviction that faith and reason, religion and science belong together.

In Chapter 4, "The organic unity of the icon and the Church ritual as a synthesis of the arts," the notion of unity is considered in a completely different context. The Wagnerian, modernist idea of the "synthesis of the arts" was voiced in Russia most famously by Vasilii Kandinsky, the abstract painter and a colleague of Florensky's for a short while at RAKhN. Florensky applied this idea in a rather unexpected fashion. It is the Church's ritual which brings together, in organic unity, the singing of the choir, the movement of the priests, the light of the candles, and the holy icons, that becomes the supreme example of synthesis. From the point of view of Russian religious philosophy, Soviet cultural policies on religious art came down to the violent disruption of the unity between the religious and the secular. The chapter raises, once again, important issues about the nature of the experience of the viewer before an icon, which Kantian aesthetics has failed to explain.

Notes

1 The phrase was popularized especially by Hent de Vries, *Philosophy and the Turn to Religion* (Baltimore, 1999).

Introduction 17

2 W.J.T. Mitchell coined the term in 1994 in his *Picture Theory: Essays on Verbal and Visual Representation* (Chicago and London, 1994).
3 The expression comes from James Elkins, *The Object Stares Back: On the Nature of Seeing* (New York and London, 1996).
4 I am borrowing the phrase from Rowan Williams's book on Dostoevsky (see Rowan Williams, *Dostoevsky: Language, Faith, and Fiction* (Waco, TX, 2011).
5 There is enormous literature on the subject. On the different connotations of "secularism" and related terms, see Karel Dobbelaere, *Secularization: A Multi-Dimensional Concept* (Beverly Hills, CA, 1981); David Martin, *The Religious and the Secular* (New York, 1969), especially chapters: "Secularization: The Range of Meaning" and "Towards Eliminating the Concept of Secularization." I have found useful the recent work by Charles Taylor – his *A Secular Age* (Cambridge, MA and London, 2007), also "What Is Secularism?" in Geoffrey Levey and Tariq Modood (eds.), *Secularism, Religion, and Multicultural Citizenship* (Cambridge, 2009), pp. xi–xxii.
6 After the book by Nicholas Zernov, *The Russian Religious Renaissance of the Twentieth Century* (New York, 1963).
7 For a good overview of some of Florensky's major ideas, see Christoph Schneider's chapter on Florensky in *The Oxford Handbook of Russian Religious Thought* (forthcoming in 2019). I have paid some attention to Florensky's ideas and their reception in Russia in my "Changing Perceptions of Pavel Florensky in Russian and Soviet Scholarship" in Sergei Oushakine and Costica Bradatan (eds.), *In Marx's Shadow: Knowledge, Power, and Intellectuals in Eastern Europe and Russia* (Lanham, 2010), pp. 73–95.
8 Avril Pyman, *Pavel Florensky: A Quiet Genius: The Tragic and Extraordinary Life of Russia's Unknown da Vinci* (New York, 2010).
9 Pavel Florensky, *The Pillar and Ground of the Truth: An Essay in Orthodox Theodicy in Twelve Letters* (1914), intro. Richard Gustafson, tr. Boris Jakim (Princeton, 1997, rpt. 2004).
10 Cited in Nicoletta Misler, "Towards an Exact Aesthetics: Pavel Florensky and the Russian Academy for Artistic Sciences" in John Bowlt and Olga Matich (eds.), *Laboratory of Dreams: The Russian Avant-Garde and Cultural Experiment* (Stanford, 1996), p. 119.
11 Pavel Florensky, "*Ob odnoi predposilke mirovozreniia*" (Of a Prerequisite of a Worldview) (1904), *Vesy*, number 9, 1904; rpt. in his *Sobranie sochineniia* (Collected Works), vol.1 (Moscow, 1994), p. 71; my translation.
12 The Moscow School of Mathematics fared particularly badly. Almost all the main figures were repressed, in one way or another. Egorov, one of the founders, was not allowed to practise his religious observances when imprisoned. He went on a hunger strike and died as a result.
13 The full title of Pyman's biography plays on a comparison between Leonardo da Vinci and Florensky, made already during Florensky's own time, as in an article by V. Filinsky, a contemporary of Florensky's (Filinsky, V., "A Russian Leonardo da Vinci in a Concentration Camp," cited in Nikolai Lossky, *History of Russian Philosophy* (London, 1952), p. 176.
14 For instance, this is the rendition of George Kline in his translation of Zenkovsky's book, as well as the translation of Alexander Schmemann's edited volume, *Ultimate Questions: An Anthology of Modern Russian Religious Thought* (London and Oxford, 1965), p. 4.

18 *Introduction*

15 Robert Slesinski prefers to use "pan-unity" (See his "The Metaphysics of Pan-Unity" in P.A. Florensky: A Worldview" in Michael Hagemeister and Nina Kauchtchtschwili (eds.), *P.A. Florenskii i kul'tura ego vremeni* (P.A. Florensky and the Culture of His Time) (Marburg, 1995), pp. 467–475).
16 Alexei Khomiakov and Ivan Kireevsky, *On Spiritual Unity*, tr. and ed. B. Jakim and R. Bird (Hudson, New York, 1998).
17 I thank Nicholas Wolterstorff (Yale University) for discussing this issue with me.
18 Vladimir Akulinin, *Filosofiia vseedinstva: Ot V.S. Solovieva k P.A. Florenskomu* (The Philosophy of Full Unity: From V.S. Soloviev to P.A. Florensky) (Novosibirsk, 1990), p. 3; my translation.
19 Ibid., p. 7.
20 Ibid., p. 13.
21 Nikolai Berdyeav, *The Russian Idea* (New York, 1948), p. 159.
22 Vasilii Zenkovsky, *A History of Russian Philosophy*, tr. G. Kline (New York and London, 1953).
23 Especially, Soloviev's *Principles of Integral Knowledge* (1877), but also in earlier works.
24 Ivan Kireevsky, "On the Nature of European Culture and on Its Relationship to Russian Culture" (1852) in Khomiakov and Kireevsky, *On Spiritual Unity*, p. 223.
25 Ibid., p. 193.
26 Ivan Kireevsky, "On the Necessity and Possibility of New Principles of Philosophy" in Khomiakov and Kireevsky, *On Spiritual Unity*, p. 240.
27 Vladimir Soloviev, *Sobranie sochineniia* (Collected Works), 10 vols. (St. Petersburg, 1911–1914), pp. 290–291; my translation.
28 For some of the origins of "full unity" in the Western tradition, see Martin Jay, "The Discourse of Totality before Western Marxism" in his *Marxism and Totality* (Cambridge and Oxford, 1984), pp. 21–81.
29 For the role of the German romantics in Russian intellectual history, see Isiah Berlin's essay, "German Romanticism in St. Petersburg and Moscow" in his *Russian Thinkers* (1948, rpt. Harmondsworth, 1978), pp. 136–156. According to Berlin, in the second half of the nineteenth century Eastern Europe and Russia were "in effect, intellectual dependencies of Germany" (p. 136). On the influence of romantic philosophy on Florensky in particular, see my "'Beauty Will Save the World': The Revival of Romantic Theories of the Symbol in Pavel Florensky's Works," *Slavonica*, vol.4/1, 2008, pp. 44–56.
30 Georg F. Hegel, *The Phenomenology of Spirit*, tr. A. Miller (Oxford, 1979), p. 11.
31 See Alexander Avramov, "*Otsenka filosofii Platona v russkoi idealisticheskoi filosofii*" (An Assessment of Plato's Philosophy in Russian Idealist Philosophy) in *Platon i ego epokha* (Plato and His Epoch) (Moscow, 1979), pp. 212–238.
32 For the notion of *holon*, see Francis Peters, *Greek Philosophical Terms* (New York, 1967), pp. 84ff. Also, G.N.G. Orsini, "The Ancient Roots of a Modern Idea" in George S. Rousseau (ed.), *Organic Form: The Life of an Idea* (London and Boston, 1972).
33 For the controversial appropriation of Spinoza by Soloviev, see Andrei Maidansky, "*Amor caucus*: Soloviev Draws Spinoza" in Teresa Obolevitch and Pawel Rojek (eds.), *Faith and Reason in Russian Thought* (Krakow, 2015).
34 Jay, "The Discourse of Totality before Western Marxism," p. 30.
35 Cited in Zenkovsky, *A History of Russian Philosophy*, pp. 481–482.
36 Florensky largely made his reputation, almost overnight, with the publication of the revised version of his Master's thesis from the Moscow Theological

Introduction   19

Academy, *Stolp i utverzhdenie istini* (The Pillar and the Ground of Truth) (Moscow, 1914).
37 Pavel Florensky, "*Razum i dialektika*" (Reason and Dialectics) (1912) in Akulinin, *Filosofiia vseedinstva* (The Philosophy of Full Unity) (Novosibirsk, 1990), p. 153; my translation.
38 Ibid., p. 155.
39 Cited in "*Zhizn' i sudba*" (Life and Fate) in Pavel Florensky (ed.), *Sochineniia v chetirekh tomakh* (Works in Four Volumes) (Moscow, 1994), p. 8; English translation in Nicoletta Misler, "Florensky as an Art Historian" in Pavel Florensky (ed.), *Beyond Vision: Essays on the Perception of Art*, ed. N. Misler (London, 2002), p. 75.
40 Ibid., p. 35; ibid., p. 56.
41 Florensky had already written poetry, which can be described as Symbolist, in his younger days.
42 Interestingly, Schopenhauer mentions the same idea, when he writes that "all primary thought takes places in pictures" (Arthur Schopenhauer, *The World as Will and Idea* (London, 1883, rpt. 1964), p. 141).
43 Pavel Florensky, *Iconostas* (Iconostasis) in Pavel Florensky, *Bogoslovskie trudy* (Theological Studies) (Moscow, 1972), p. 134.
44 Ibid., my italics.
45 Florensky's essay was published by the famous Russian journal, *Trudy po znakovim sistemam* (Researches on Sign Systems), the main organ of the Moscow-Tartu School of Semiotics (see vol.3, 1967, pp. 381–346). Boris Uspensky, one of the main figures of the Moscow-Tartu School of Semiotics, has been instrumental in popularizing Florensky's theory of the icon both in Russia and in the West. He wrote the introductory article to Florensky's essay on "reverse perspective" when it was published in *Trudy po znakovim sistemam* (Researches on Sign Systems). Uspensky's book, *The Semiotics of the Russian Icon*, which has been translated into several languages is itself strongly influenced by Florensky (see Boris Uspensky, *The Semiotics of the Russian Icon* (Lisse, 1976)). The Italian scholar Nicoletta Misler has published widely on Florensky's writings on art. She also edited and wrote the introduction to the collection of Florensky's articles on art, translated into English (see Florensky, *Beyond Vision*).
46 I have researched particularly the problem of "reverse perspective" of which Florensky is the main exponent (see my joint paper with Martin Kemp, " 'Reverse Perspective': Historical Fallacies and an Alternative View" in Michele Emmer (ed.), *The Visual Mind II* (Cambridge, MA, 2005), pp. 399–433; "On the Problem of 'Reverse Perspective': Definitions East and West," *Leonardo*, vol.43/5, 2010, pp. 464–470; *Space, Time, and Presence in the Icon: Seeing the World with the Eyes of God* (Farnham, 2010).
47 See Misler's "Florensky as an Art Historian" in her introduction to Florensky, *Beyond Vision*.
48 Evgeny Trubetskoy, *Umozrenie v kraskakh: tri ocherka o russkoi ikone* (Contemplation in Colours: Three Articles on the Russian Icon) (Paris, 1965).
49 Sergei Bulgakov, *Ikona i ikonopochitanie* (Icon and Icon-worship) (Paris, 1931).
50 Sergei Khoruzii, "*Filosofii simvolizm P.A. Florenskogo i ego zhiznenie iztoki*" (P.A. Florensky's Philosophy of Symbolism and Its Living Sources) in Konstantin Isupov (ed.), *P. A. Florenskii: Pro et contra* (St. Petersburg, 1996), p. 528.
51 Pavel Florensky, "*Avtobiograficheskaia statiia*" (Autobiographical Article) (1927) in *Entsiklopedicheskii slovar' Russkogo Bibliograficheskogo institute 'Granat'*

20 *Introduction*

(Encyclopaedic Dictionary of the Russian Bibliographical Institute "Granat"), vol.44 (Moscow, 1927), p. 144.
52 Pavel Florensky, *Detiam moim* (1923) (Moscow, 1992), p. 152; my translation.
53 John of Damascus, *On the Divine Images* (Crestwood, New York, 1980).
54 I have found most useful James Elkins's *On the Strange Place of Religion in Contemporary Art* (New York and London, 2004) and Paul Crowther's *How Pictures Complete Us: The Beautiful, the Sublime, and the Divine* (Stanford, 2016). Crowther considers the problem of the icon specifically in his chapter entitled "From Perspective to the Icon: Marion's Theology of Painting."
55 Communication from Jeremy Begbie, formerly director of the project "Theology through the Arts" at the universities of Cambridge and of St. Andrews. See Jeremy Begbie, *Theology, Music, and Time* (Cambridge, 2000); Nicholas Wolterstorff, *Art in Action: Toward a Christian Aesthetic* (Grand Rapids, 1980).
56 Erwin Panofsky, *Gothic Architecture and Scholasticism* (Latrobe, PA, 1951, several rpts. since).
57 In his *Einleitung in die monumentale Theologie* (1867).
58 For a discussion of Piper, see Jeffrey Hamburger, "The Place of Theology in Medieval Art History" in Jeffrey Hamburger (ed.), *The Mind's Eye: Art and Theological Argument in the Middle Ages* (Princeton, 2006), pp. 18–19.
59 Charles Barber, *Figure and Likeness: On the Limits of Representation in Byzantine Iconoclasm* (Princeton and Oxford, 2002), p. 53.
60 Ibid.
61 In my *Space, Time, and Presence in the Icon*.
62 Robin Cormack, *Painting the Soul* (London, 1997), p. 112.
63 The most useful studies looking at this problem in a constructive way are very probably Martin Kemp's series of articles in the journal *Nature*. Some of the articles are collected in Martin Kemp, *Vizualization: The Nature Book of Art and Science* (Oxford and New York, 2001). Notice Kemp's concept of "structural intuitions," i.e. the idea that there are structures that "are both those of the intuitive processes themselves and those of the external features whose structures are being intuited" (p. 1).
64 Taylor, *A Secular Age*, p. 535.
65 Jose Casanova, *Public Religions in the Modern World* (Chicago and London, 1994), p. 5.
66 See Thomas Luckmann, *Invisible Religion* (New York, 1967).
67 Jürgen Habermas, "Religion in the Public Sphere," *European Journal of Philosophy*, vol.14/1, 2006, p. 13.
68 Taylor, *A Secular Age*, pp. 31, 473; the italics are mine.
69 Ibid., p. 12.
70 Ibid., p. 18.
71 Peter Berger, *The Social Reality of Religion* (London, 1980).
72 Soren Kierkegaard, *Concluding Unscientific Postscript* (1846) (London, 1945), p. 223.
73 Nowadays, Richard Dawkins has gone to great lengths to prove that "you can be an atheist who is happy, balanced, moral, and intellectually fulfilled" (Richard Dawkins, *The God Delusion* (London, 2006), p. 23).
74 Paul Tillich, *Art and Architecture* (New York, 1987), p. 173. On the connotations of the term "religion," see also Jonathan Z. Smith, "A Matter of Class: Taxonomies of Religion," *Harvard Theological Review*, vol.89/4, 1996, pp. 387–403.

Introduction 21

75 Vladimir Fedorov, "*Predislovie: Pavel Florensky kak missioner XXI veka*" (Preface: Pavel Florensky as a Missionary of the Twenty-First Century) in *Pamiati Pavla Florenskogo* (In Memory of Pavel Florensky) (St. Petersburg, 2002), p. 8.
76 Natalia Bonetskaia in Johannes Schelhas, "Florensky Today: Three Points of View," *Russian Studies in Philosophy*, vol.40/4, Spring 2002, p. 85.
77 George Florovsky, *Puti russkogo bogosloviia* (The Paths of Russian Theology) (Paris, 1937), p. 495.
78 Zenkovsky, *A History of Russian Philosophy*, p. 880.
79 This is the account of Nikolay Lossky, a prominent Russian émigré philosopher, who refers specifically to the impact of Florensky's *The Pillar and the Ground of Truth* (Nikolai Lossky, *History of Russian Philosophy* (London, 1950), p. 177. See also Luzin, one of the founders of the Moscow School of Mathematics, who writes in a letter about the "overwhelming impression" of *The Pillar*: "As I read it I was stunned the entire time as by blows from battering ram" (Cited in Loren Graham and Jean-Michel Kantor, *Naming Infinity* (Cambridge, MA and London, 2009), p. 83).
80 Steven Bruce, *Religion in the Modern World* (Oxford, 1996), p. 4.
81 Tillich, *Art and Architecture*, p. 172.
82 Vries's book deals exclusively with continental philosophers (Vries, *Philosophy and the Turn to Religion*). Nicholas Wolterstorff has attracted attention to the "turn to religion" in analytical philosophy (Nicholas Wolterstorff, "The Religious Turn in Philosophy and Art" in Ludwig Nagl (ed.), *Religion nach der Religionskritik* (Wien, 2003), pp. 273–283).
83 Jürgen Habermas and Joseph Ratzinger, *The Dialectics of Secularization: On Reason and Religion* (San Francisco, 2005), p. 38.
84 Habermas, "Religion in the Public Sphere," p. 16.
85 For instance, see Philip Blond, *Post-secular Philosophy* (London, 1998).
86 See, for example, John Milbank, *Theology and Social Theory: Beyond Secular Reason* (Oxford, 1990); Avishai Margalit and Moshe Halbertal, *Idolatry* (Cambridge, MA, 1992); Talal Asad, *Genealogies of Religion: Discipline and Reasons of Power in Christianity and Islam* (Baltimore, 1993). More recently and up to the present, we see works by Charles Taylor and Habermas, but also Veit Bader, José Casanova, Rajeev Bhargava, Tariq Modood, etc.
87 There is mention of this in Alexander Agadjanian, "Breakthrough to Modernity, Apologia for Traditionalism: The Russian Orthodox View of Society and Culture in Comparative Perspective," *Religion, State, and Society*, vol.31, 2003, p. 338.
88 For example, Paul Heelas, Linda Woodhead, et al., *The Spiritual Revolution* (Oxford, 2004), p. 24.
89 There is a useful and accessible account of "communitarian" philosophy in Lachezar Antonov, *Critique of Monological Reason* (Blagoevgrad, 2011) (in Bulgarian). See also Will Kymlicka, *Liberalism, Community, and Culture* (Oxford, 1989); Shlomo Anneri and Avner de-Shalit (eds.), *Communitarianism and Individualism* (Oxford, 1992); David Bell, *Communitarianism and Its Critics* (Oxford, 1993).

1 The unity of man and God before the icon
The icon as "energetic symbol"

In a highly intimate text addressed to his children, Florensky wrote: "All my life I have been thinking about one thing – about the relation between phenomenon and noumenon."[1] That relation, according to Florensky, is to be understood through the symbol. We are surrounded by symbols: i.e. phenomena that reveal and even "contain" the noumena, for "the mystery of the world is not hidden, but is precisely revealed through symbols in its true essence – that is, as a mystery."[2] Clearly, "symbol" is interpreted here as possessing a unifying function; i.e. it brings about the unity of the phenomenon and the noumenon, of the immanent and the transcendent. This connotation of the term goes back to the ancient Greek *symbolon*, from the verb *symballein*, which means "to throw together, to unite, to fit together,"[3] in this case to unite what belongs to our immanent world to what belongs to the higher, transcendent world. Integral knowledge becomes very much the ability of recognizing the symbols in the phenomena.

The view of the symbol as the unity of the immanent and the transcendent has had a long history in human thought. In this chapter, I will address only one moment of this history, namely the understanding of the visual image as symbol, which was vigorously promoted by Florensky throughout the corpus of his writings. The Russian thinker drew from several major sources, including the Byzantine theology of the icon and the German romantic opposition between symbol and allegory. I have paid more detailed attention to both the Byzantine and the German background elsewhere.[4] The common element in these diverse intellectual influences is the idea that the visual image is a symbol in the sense that it "contains" the presence of the depicted being or figure. The symbol *is* the symbolized. Thus, the icon of Christ (immanent) *is* Christ (transcendent) in a manner defined by the Byzantine iconophile theologians of the eighth and ninth centuries.

In the following text I would like to draw attention to a little-known aspect of Florensky's preoccupation with the symbol. I will suggest that the Russian writer's works on the visual image, mostly from the 1920s, present a

The unity of man and God before the icon 23

further stage in earlier work, mostly from the 1910s, on the philosophy of the language and specifically the philosophy of the Name. More concretely, Florensky became arguably the most intellectually influential figure in the *imiaslavie* (Name-Worshipping) controversy, which unfolded particularly in and after 1913. By defending the *imiaslavtsy* (the followers of Name-Worshipping) in his writings, he went back to the terminology and positions expressed by the fourteenth-century Byzantine theologian St. Gregory Palamas and particularly Palamas's theology of divine essence and energies. This work, I believe, lies at the heart of Florensky's later definition of the icon as "energetic symbol." There is a smooth and logical transition between the idea that "the Name of God is God" in terms of divine energies (but not essence) and the notion that the icon of Christ discloses the energies (and, again, not the essence) of Christ and is, therefore, Christ Himself.

My purpose in this instance is not simply to point out yet another intellectual source of Florensky's theory of the image. Rather, I would like to demonstrate through a particular example what I believe to be an approach to knowledge which is highly typical of Florensky's thinking. The pretext is frequently a concrete contemporary issue – in this case, the Name-Worshipping controversy in Russia. Florensky analyzes this issue by placing it within the long history of Eastern Orthodox Christian thought. The familiar theological dogmas and ideas, such as the Palamite distinction between divine essence and energies, are, however, thoroughly modernized exactly by drawing the visual implications which lay dormant in medieval theology. This is how Palamite terminology, meant to describe the relationship between God and man, is used to describe this relationship in the specific case when it takes place before the icon.

The *imiaslavtsy* incident in 1913 and its intellectual afterlife

In June 1913, the monks of Mount Athos, the greatest conglomerate of Orthodox monasteries in the world, were subjected to an unusual sight. Right before their eyes they could see military ships approaching their tranquil surroundings. To their great astonishment, they realized that the Russian Navy meant to storm the Russian monastery of St. Panteleimon on the Mount, on the grounds that some of the monks belonged to the movement of *imiaslavie* ("Name-Worshipping" or "Name-glorifying" in English), which the Holy Synod of the Russian Orthodox Church had declared heretical. The monks, who refused to recant, were arrested and sent back to Russia, where they were excommunicated.

The incident could be dismissed as yet another row between monks and church officials if it were not for its hugely important and surprisingly wide-ranging impact in a number of intellectual contexts. Indeed,

Name-Worshipping left a deep imprint on religious philosophy, but also – and probably more surprisingly – on developments in mathematics. A recent study has suggested that Name-Worshipping was "instrumental in helping the birth of a new field of modern mathematics,"[5] i.e. what is known as Descriptive Set Theory, developed by the world-famous Moscow School of Mathematics in the 1920s and 1930s. One of the founders of the school, the great mathematician Dmitrii Egorov, was a practising Name-Worshipper.[6] It was Florensky, however, a member of the school, who systematically applied mathematical ideas to theological and religious problems, which emerged in the *imiaslavie* debates (See Chapter 3, section "Florensky and the development of a mathematical worldview"). In this sense, his use of the same theological ideas in his theory of the icon should be seen as a consistent approach of using creatively – and sometimes controversially, as we will see – theological notions in completely new and frequently unexpected contexts.

The drama on the Holy Mountain had been provoked by a revival of the Hesychast practice of the Jesus prayer and the accompanying belief that the Name of God, recited during the prayer, was God Himself. Hesychasm was a mystical movement in medieval Byzantium, whose theological importance was mainly due to the writings of St. Gregory Palamas (1296–1359), a monk from Mount Athos who became the Archbishop of Thessaloniki. In the process of defending Hesychast spirituality, St. Gregory developed a sophisticated theology which is a cornerstone of Eastern Orthodox thought. It is well-known that Hesychasm had a strong following in medieval Russia; there has been an interesting debate among scholars on the possible impact of Hesychasm particularly on fourteenth and fifteenth century Russian religious painting.[7] The Hesychast revival in nineteenth century Russia has also attracted significant attention.[8] In this sense, the incident with the Russian monks on Mount Athos bears witness to yet another revival of Hesychasm in Russian history.

Interestingly, rather than extinguishing the movement the events on Mount Athos in 1913 gave it intellectual credibility. The issuing controversy touched on, sometimes gave focus to, many of the themes that lay at the heart of the full unity movement. Some of the foremost thinkers at the time got involved (Sergei Bulgakov, Vladimir Ern, later Alexei Losev), while arguably no one's intellectual impact was as important as Florensky's. Florensky's role was crucial in defining the dominant framework within which the controversy was interpreted at the time and since. Indeed, it was Florensky who established the implicit opposition between the mysticism and genuine spiritual experience of the *imiaslatsy* and the rationalism and positivism of their opponents.[9] In his notes, written at the time and not meant for publication,[10] he describes the conflict as a philosophical struggle between the Platonic idealism of the Name-Worshippers and "the Kantian positivistic point of view" of their opponents.[11] For Florensky, the whole debate was of the utmost importance, because it came down to the possibility or impossibility of a union between man and God. To deny the possibility that the Name of God was God was to deny the possibility of a communion between God and man. It is through the divine energies in the Name that man finds himself, quite literally, in the presence of God.

It should be kept in mind that while Hesychasm as a movement had an almost uninterrupted history in Russia, the theology of St. Gregory Palamas – whose teaching provided the main theological support of Hesychast spirituality – was largely forgotten in nineteenth-century Russia. Tellingly, both versions of the *Philokalia* (the standard collection of texts on Eastern Orthodox Hesychast theology, first compiled in the eighteenth century) – by Paisii Velichkovski at the end of the eighteenth century and by Feofan Zatvornik (or Theophan the Recluse) in the nineteenth century – omit Palamas's theological writings.[12] This is remarkable, considering that Palamas's teaching had been part of the official doctrine of the Orthodox Church as a result of the decisions of two important councils in the fourteenth century. During the *imiaslavie* debates in the 1910s it became clear that, as Scott Kenworthy remarks, "no one in the debate had actually read Palamas, nor were they familiar with the fourteenth-century councils."[13] We encounter, therefore, the interesting situation whereby theologians and philosophers who did not know Palamas's works in the original were consistently using terminology which is clearly Palamite. Florensky was no exception, while the same applies to Sergei Bulgakov and Vladimir Ern. While Florensky refers in passing to the Byzantine theologian in his *Pillar and Ground of Truth*, his citations are almost invariably from secondary sources. At the same time, as we will see, both in his works on the Name-worshippers and in his writings on the icon, Florensky relies heavily on terms that are clearly Palamite.

Already in the nineteenth century, when Kireevsky maintained that integral knowledge was possible only "because the energies communicate a full image of being,"[14] I believe that he used the term "energy" exactly in the sense of Palamas. In this way, while there was little familiarity with St. Gregory's works in the original, Palamite energetism became an important influence on the Russian philosophy of full unity from the very beginning. It was the controversies around the Russian Name-worshippers, however, that pushed Palamas into the spotlight. In many ways, this was the immediate background of the works of Vladimir Lossky and John Meyendorff that put Palamite teaching firmly on the map of modern Eastern Orthodox theology. In the following section, I will focus on Florensky's highly original application of Palamite theological terminology to the theory of the icon.

From word to image: drawing the visual implications of Palamism

One of the purposes of this chapter is to show that, for Florensky, one of the sites of the encounter between God and man, an idea of immense importance in Orthodox theology, takes place before the icon. The experience of the believer before the holy image is conceptualized by Florensky through his application of Palamite terminology. Ultimately, the Russian author defines the Orthodox icon as an "energetic symbol" (*energiinii simvol*).

The distinction between essence and energies, which St. Gregory Palamas is known for, goes back to Aristotle (especially in the *Metaphysics*). In Aristotelian philosophy, a thing is said to consist of essence (*ousia*) and energy (*energeia*). All entities interpenetrate through their energies (but not their essences!) and these reciprocal relationships constitute the full unity of being. From pagan philosophy, Aristotle's terminology entered Christian theology and became a belief fundamental to the Eastern Church.[15] As the profession of faith, worked out at the Council of Nicaea I (325) demonstrates, the three hypostases of the Godhead share "essence" (or "substance"):

> We believe [. . .] in the one Lord Jesus Christ, Son of God, only-begotten, born of the Father, God of God, Light of Light, true God of the true God, born, not made, of one substance with the Father, through whom all things are made.

In other words, God the Father and Jesus are "consubstantial" as they share the same substance or essence (*ousia*). At the same time, the Church Fathers such as St. Athanasius drew a distinction between divine essence and God's powers and bounty. In the eighth century, St. John of Damascus wrote about the actions or "energies" of God as revelations of God Himself.

Following in the footsteps of Greek Patristic theology and combining the doctrine of divine actions worked out in the Christological controversies and the doctrine of divine essence from the Trinitarian debates,[16] St. Gregory Palamas applies the distinction between essence and energy to God and His relationship to man. In the spirit of apophatic theology, he stresses over and over again that God is absolutely unknowable in His essence. This is an idea especially familiar from the Cappadocian Fathers and St. John Chrysostom. At the same time, God makes Himself accessible to us in His energies. According to Palamas, "God is one, He is at the same time incomprehensible (*akateleptos*) in His essence and comprehensible in His energies."[17] This means that God is constituted of one essence, three hypostases, and also uncreated energy. It also means that God exists in his essence and outside it at the same time.[18] The two highly important Councils of Constantinople, in 1341 and in 1351, confirmed the Orthodoxy of Palamas's position and proclaimed the distinction between "essence" and "grace." According to the formulations of the Councils, the energies proceed from God and manifest His own Being.

It is in this sense – which is theologically correct – that one should understand Florensky's writings on Name-Worshipping. The frequently repeated Hesychast formula "the Name of God is God Himself" (*Imia Bozhie est' Sam Bog*) is true in so far as the Name is a symbol which "contains" the divine energies. In his text, "Name-Worshipping as a Philosophical Premise," written in 1913 in direct response to the *imiaslavtsy* incident, Florensky defined the symbol in recognizably Palamite terms: "a symbol is an essence energy of what is joined, or, more precisely commingled, with the energy of another essence, more worthy in a given respect, and which thereby carries this other essence in itself."[19] The compound term "essence energy" is used in the Palamite sense of energy which flows out of the essence (see St. Gregory's *Triads*).

There is a recognizable Orthodox theological background to Florensky's understanding of the symbol as "something that manifests in itself that which is not itself, that which is greater than itself and is nevertheless essentially manifested through itself."[20] Once again, St. Gregory Palamas comes to mind, this time with his definition of a "natural" symbol. In the *Triads* and other works, St. Gregory distinguishes between "created" and "natural" symbols.[21] A natural symbol accompanies what it symbolizes as in the example of the dawn which accompanies the rising sun and the heat – the burning power of fire (*Triads* III.I.14). As Palamas writes, "the capacity of the fire to burn, which has as its symbol heat accessible to the senses, becomes its own symbol, for it is always accompanied by this heat, yet remains one and does not exist as a double" (*Triads* III.I.20). The paradigmatic case would be God, Who, in the words of Maximus the Confessor, in the Incarnation "became His own symbol" (*Ambigua* 10 in *PG* 91 1165D).

A closeness between St. Gregory Palamas and Florensky can be noticed on another level. Both embraced the dialectical dimension of the relationship between essence and energy. In fact, both writers saw the ability to believe two things, which might be contradictory in formal logic, at the same time as essential to Eastern Orthodox thought. Thus, the Name of God is at the same time God (God is present in His Name through His energies) and not (God is not present in His essence). As St. Gregory said, it is as vital to realize that God's essence is unattainable even to the angels and is beyond all categories of thought as it is to believe in the accessibility of divine energies. Further he maintained that "to say now one thing [in this case, God is knowable] and now another [God is unknowable] is natural to any man who would theologize aright."[22] Orthodoxy, for Palamas, becomes "the capacity to observe both aspects of a truth that was dialectical," while heresy is "not so much the outright denial of dogma as the adherence to one pole of a dialectical dogma at the expense of the other pole."[23] The same dialectical thrust of thought characterizes Florensky's philosophical position, which views integral knowledge as possible only via the antinomical structure of the human mind, since Truth itself is profoundly antinomical.[24] Therefore, "the characteristic feature of dogma is precisely in that it demands the overcoming (*preodolenie*) of reason for the faith in it. Where there is no contradiction to reason – there is nothing to believe."[25] In the Letter on "Contradiction" in his *The Pillar and the Ground of Truth* (1914), Florensky cites Nicholas of Cusa, who famously defined Truth as *coincidentia oppositorum*, i.e. the coincidence of opposites. Thus, Florensky was perfectly comfortable in defining the Name and later the icon in similar terms. Both the Divine Name and the icon are symbols and as such both are the symbolized and are not.

Interestingly, on the rare occasions when St. Gregory Palamas referred specifically to icons, he never used the essence–energies terminology. In his *Confession of the Orthodox Faith*, for example, he takes up the issue of the relationship between icon and prototype and explains: "we venerate [. . .] the holy image of the Son of God who has been depicted as made man for our sake, referring the veneration relatively to the prototype." Further, he adds that "in the same manner we venerate also the images of all the saints." "In the veneration of images," he summarizes, we carry our thoughts "to the forms of the images."[26] The terminology here was developed by the Iconophile theologians during the Byzantine Iconoclastic Controversy (8th–9th c.). In other words, it was Florensky, not Palamas, who saw the usefulness of the application of the essence–energies distinction for the theology of the icon.

Already in Florensky's writings on *imiaslavie*, there are passages that make the connection between the Name of God and the icon. In other words, at times Florensky's philosophy of language spills over into a concern with the visual image. For example, at one point the Russian author explicitly says that the Divine Names "are" God in the same way in which an image of Peter is Peter. When one looks at the icon of Peter one says "this is Peter," not "this is the picture of Peter."[27] Indeed, in several parts of his texts on *imiaslavie* Florensky mentions that Names share a common feature with images and symbols in that they have a real connection to what they signify – and this is important because otherwise we would have no way of knowing the signified at all.[28] Another trope that comes up at the crossroads of discussions on word and image is that of the "window" (that opens from the immanent to the transcendent world), a theme in much of the Byzantine theology of the icon. We see Florensky using it in connection to the Name, no doubt fully aware of its original use in the theology of the image. Thus, he refers to the "window" as being open when one calls upon God in the process of prayer.[29] In his later texts on the icon, as we will see, he goes back to the "window" metaphor.

In his works from the 1920s, Florensky applied his thinking on the Name of God and the Jesus prayer to the visual image much more consistently. In his *Iconostasis* (1922), he defined the icon as identical with the prototype and as different from it at the same time. On the one hand, an icon discloses the presence of the person or the being depicted. As Florensky says:

> Now I look at an icon and I say to myself: "Behold, this is She" – not Her picture, but She Herself, contemplated by means of, with the aid of, iconographic art. As through a window, I see the Mother of God.[30]

On the other hand, however, the icon "on its own" – i.e. apart from the spiritual vision – "is neither an image nor an icon, but a wooden board."[31] The Russian writer clarifies this antinomy by going back to the example of the window, which on its own is no more than "wood and glass," but once we are able to see the light through it, then it becomes "that very light itself" and not just "like the light."[32] In a passage that brings together the two themes – the Name of God and the icon – he states that: "I acquired the basic thought of my worldview: what is named in name, what is symbolized in the symbol, the reality of what is pictured in the picture, is indeed present."[33]

It is interesting that in his writings on the icon from the 1920s,[34] Florensky uses language that lends itself naturally to visualization. There is the persistent theme of the "boundary" – Florensky has been called, quite rightly, "a philosopher of the boundary"[35] – and the related notion of crossing the boundary in an upward movement (ascent) and downward movement (descent). The movement of ascent implies crossing from our immanent reality to the transcendent reality of God and vice versa, descent is the downward movement that brings us back to our own world. The symbol belongs to this boundary zone. Therefore, icons as symbols become "the visible witnesses of the invisible world,"[36] they "dwell simultaneously in two worlds, combining within themselves the life here and the life there."[37] They are the link between the two worlds and possess characteristics of both the transcendent and the immanent worlds. In other words, the iconic image as symbol makes present and accessible to the senses (a characteristic of this world) what is, in principle, invisible and only spirit (a characteristic of the otherworldly). The authentic icon, which fulfils its purpose, incorporates both these moments, as in Florensky's example of the image of the Mother of God, which is "not Her picture, but She Herself."

As I have proposed elsewhere, an immediate antecedent of the ascent–descent pair was very likely Viacheslav Ivanov's distinction between *liniia voskhozhdeniia* (line of ascent) and *liniia niskhozhdeniia* (line of descent). Ivanov, a prominent Symbolist poet and the major theoretical spokesman of the Russian Symbolist movement, who was a close friend of Florensky's, in turn, had probably borrowed it from Nietzsche (specifically Nietzsche's Apollonian–Dionysian opposition) to describe the process of artistic creation,[38] a connotation with strongly romantic overtones. While I still think that these sources are relevant, I have come to believe that the theological context within which they are placed by Florensky is essential to understanding the process of "Orthodoxization," to which the Russian thinker subjected practically all the material he was dealing with.

As we have seen, Florensky employed the notion of energy to describe a wide range of phenomena that go well beyond the original connotation of the term in Palamas. It is fair to acknowledge that there has been a highly critical, sometimes openly negative, reception of Florensky's views, as witnessed by the contemporary philosopher Sergei Khoruzhii, who has gone as far as to call Florensky's approach to notions deriving from St. Gregory Palamas "theological nonsense."[39] The debate is extremely complex, as it involves a number of controversial issues, including not only the nature of Florensky's borrowings from Palamas, but also the ambiguity of Palamas himself.[40] For instance, Rowan Williams has drawn attention to the problems inherent in Palamas's attempt to impose a Neo-Platonic ontology upon Christianity.[41] This is very much Khoruzhii's problem with Florensky and the whole movement, which he calls "the Moscow School of Christian Neo-Platonism," and which represents the last and final stage of the Russian movement of full unity. Losev, Sergei Bulgakov, and others – most of whom were under the strong influence of Florensky – belong to this school, which from roughly 1912 onwards put into the centre of its philosophy the relationship between essence and energy.[42]

The Orthodox theological concept of "synergy" (*synergeia*), which refers to the union of two essences, is used by Palamas specifically in reference to the union between God and man through the action of divine energies. Florensky, Khoruzhii claims, applies it to the union of any two entities.[43] Florensky does give grounds for such an interpretation, as when he says "all things are interrelated by mysterious bonds," "the energies of things impinge upon other things; each lives in all and all in each."[44] The question is if his application of Palamite ideas in each concrete case keeps to the spirit of Eastern Orthodox theology in general and the theology of St. St. Gregory Palamas in particular. The view I hold here is that Florensky's theory of the icon in particular belongs organically to Eastern Orthodox thought and is a theologically sound elaboration of Palamism. The very focus on the icon, understood exactly as a visual image, is a theme running throughout Orthodox Christianity and is the direct result of apophatic, mystical theology. Ultimately, the believer should attempt to go beyond vision, but to do so he needs the help of visual images that God, in His mercy, has provided.

In many ways, both Byzantine Palamism and the Neo-Palamism of Florensky can be interpreted as a witness to Christ's words: "Blessed are the pure in heart, for they shall see God" (Matthew 5–8). As with the whole movement of apophatic theology, which denies the possibility that God can be known through concepts, St. Gregory is committed to the view that it is contemplation and vision that lead to union with God.[45] Vision ranks above discourse (logos) in this tradition. It has been noticed that for St. Gregory Palamas, "practising and being in touch with God are detached from the theologian, but they remain constant characteristics of the one who pursues the vision of God."[46] This is why the experience of uncreated light (i.e. the light seen by the Apostles on the Mount Tabor) holds such a central place in Palamism.[47] In this way, Florensky's idea that divine energy dwells in the icon and therefore, before the icon the believer is in the presence of the figure depicted, while utterly original, is also very much in the spirit of Orthodox and particularly Palamite theology.

Conclusion and implications

In this chapter several arguments have been advanced which have wide implications, well beyond the concrete incident of the Russian Name-Worshippers, which served as my starting ground.

Firstly, I have claimed an unusual model of the reception of one author by another. The influence of St. Gregory Palamas on Florensky and other representatives of the movement of full unity came mostly indirectly, via secondary sources, and yet, if my interpretation is correct, it was profound. It was, however, exactly as a result of the debates around the Russian *imiaslavtsy* that the theological works of St. Gregory Palamas were rediscovered in Russia at the beginning of the twentieth century. We should, therefore, consider Neo-Palamism as a factor in the development of the Russian religious philosophy of full unity and the "religious renaissance" in early twentieth-century Russia. This has not been done in any systematic way yet.

Secondly, I have suggested that it was Florensky who applied the Palamite teaching on divine essence and energies to the theory of the icon. In the process, he defined the icon as an "energetic symbol," that brings about the unity of the immanent and the transcendent. By drawing from the visual implications underlying Palamite theology, Florensky makes a genuine contribution to the long line of Eastern Orthodox tradition of thought

32 *The unity of man and God before the icon*

on the theological significance of the icon and the visual. What is really valuable about Florensky's highly original reading of Palamas is that his concern with visuality was a way of articulating his concern with the crisis of modernity. What was so problematic about modern culture and modern Western philosophy – from Florensky's perspective and the perspective of the entire movement of full unity – was the disjunction between the immanent and the transcendent worlds, between the phenomenon and the noumenon. Florensky was committed to the view that the two (phenomenon and noumenon) were unified and one, as "every phenomenon expresses a spiritual essence"[48] and is, therefore, a symbol. Throughout his writings, Florensky keeps going back to the idea that what connects the phenomenon and noumenon are energies. It is in this sense that the icon is defined as an "energetic symbol," a position which is profoundly Orthodox.

Thirdly, Florensky's works on the symbol and the unity of man and God in the experience of the icon imply a completely different scopic regime to the one of Cartesian philosophy. In this way, they could provide a vital link in the process of overcoming the concept of visuality inherited from the Enlightenment and could offer a new model of visuality instead. I will, in fact, suggest that Florensky's writings on "reverse perspective" (i.e. the principle of organizing space in the medieval icon) represent a concrete alternative model to Albertian perspectivism. This will be the subject of the next chapter.

Notes

1 Florensky, *Detiam moim* (To My Children), p. 153; my translation.
2 Cited in Viktor Bychkov, *The Aesthetic Face of Being: Art in the Theology of Pavel Florensky* (Crestwood, New York, 1993), pp. 67–68.
3 See Henry Liddle, Robert Scott, Henry S. Jones, and Roderick McKenzie (eds.), *A Greek-English Lexicon*, 9th ed. (Oxford, 1925).
4 For the Byzantine theology of the icon and its influence on Florensky, see my *Space, Time, and Presence in the Icon*, esp. Chapter 3: "Registering Presence in the Icon." For the German romantic sources, see my "'Beauty Will Save the World:' The Revival of Romantic Theories of the Symbol in Pavel Florensky's Works," *Slavonica*, vol.14/1, 2008, pp. 44–56.
5 Graham and Kantor, *Naming Infinity*, p. 5.
6 Egorov was arrested in 1930. While in prison, he went on a hunger strike in protest against his being prevented from following his religious practice. He died as a result of his hunger strike.
7 See Viktor Lazarev, *Feofan Grek i ego shkola* (Theophanes the Greek and His School) (Moscow, 1979), p. 29; N.K. Goleizovsky, "Isikhazm i russkaia zhivopis' XIV–XV vv" (Hesychasm and Russian Painting of the Fourteenth and Fifteenth Centuries), *Vizantiisky vremennik*, vol.29, 1968, pp. 196–210; Mikhail Alpatov, "Iskusstvo Feofana Greka i uchenie isikhastov" (The Art of

The unity of man and God before the icon 33

Theophanes the Greek and the Teaching of the Hesychasts), *Vizantiisky vremennik*, vol.33, 1972, pp. 190–202.

8 See Scott Kenworthy, *The Heart of Russia: Trinity-Sergius, Monasticism, and Society after 1825* (Washington and New York, 2010); Irina Paert, *Spiritual Elders: Charisma and Tradition in Russian Orthodoxy* (DeKalb, 2011).

9 On this, see Scott Kenworthy, "Archbishop Nikon (Rozhdestvenskii) and Pavel Florensky on Spiritual Experience, Theology, and the Name-Glorifiers Dispute" in Judith Kornblatt and Patrick Michelson (eds.), *Thinking Orthodox in Modern Russia: Culture, History, Context* (Madison, 2014). According to Kenworthy, "much of this interpretation was shaped by Florensky."

10 The notes were first published in 1995 in *Nachala*, numbers 1–4, 1995.

11 Pavel Florensky, "*Primechaniia sviashchennika Pavla Florenskogo k stat'e arkhiepiskopa Nikona 'Velikoe izkushenie okolo sviateishego Imeni Bozhiia*," *Nachala*, numbers 1–4, 1995; rpt. Pavel Florensky, *Sochineniia v 4 tomakh* (Writings in Four Volumes), vol.3, p. 316.

12 The eighteenth-century version completely excluded Palamas, while the nineteenth-century version included none of the important theological works, but only texts describing the practice of prayer.

13 Communication from Scott Kenworthy (Havighurst Centre, Miami University, Ohio) of 6 November 2012. Kenworthy is one of the main authorities on these issues.

14 Khomiakov and Kireevsky, *On Spiritual Unity*.

15 For a genealogy of the distinction, see Rowan Williams, "The Philosophical Structures of Palamism," *Eastern Churches Review*, vol.9, 1977, pp. 27–44. For its importance in Orthodox Christianity, see Vladimir Lossky, *The Mystical Theology of the Eastern Church* (Cambridge, 1957); Christos Yannaras, "The Distinction between Essence and Energy and Its Importance for Theology," *St. Vladimir's Theological Quarterly*, vol.19, 1975, pp. 232–245; Kallistos Ware, "God Hidden and Revealed: The Apophatic Way and the Essence-Energies Distinction," *Eastern Churches Review*, vol.7, 1975, pp. 125–136.

16 See George Florovsky, "St. Gregory Palamas and the Tradition of the Fathers," *Sobornost*, vol.4, 1961, pp. 165–176; also Jaroslav Pelikan, *The Christian Tradition*, vol.2: *The Spirit of Eastern Christendom* (Chicago and London, 1974), p. 269.

17 Cited in George Papademetriou, *Introduction to St. Gregory Palamas* (New York, 1973), p. 34.

18 Lossky, *The Mystical Theology of the Eastern Church*, p. 71.

19 Pavel Florensky, "*Imeslavie kak filosofskaia predposilka*" (Name-Worshipping as a Philosophical Premise) (1913), English translation from Bychkov, *The Aesthetic Face of Being*, p. 70.

20 Ibid., p. 70.

21 On this, see David Bradshaw, *Aristotle East and West: Metaphysics and the Division of Christendom* (Cambridge, 2004), pp. 236 ff.

22 Cited in Pelikan, *The Christian Tradition*, vol.2: *The Spirit of Eastern Christendom*, p. 264.

23 Ibid.

24 On this see Robert Slesinski, *Pavel Florensky: A Metaphysics of Love* (Crestwood, New York,1984), pp. 63 and 140 ff and Christoph Schneider, "'Will the Truth not Demand a Sacrifice from Us?' Reflections on Pavel A. Florensky's

34 The unity of man and God before the icon

Idea of Truth as Antinomy in *The Pillar and Ground of Truth* (1914)," *Sobornost*, vol.34/2, 2013, pp. 34–51.
25 Florensky, "*Primechaniia sviashchennika Pavla Florenskogo*," rpt. Florensky, *Sochineniia v 4 tomakh* (Writings in Four Volumes), p. 300.
26 St. Gregory Palamas, "Confession of the Orthodox Faith" in J. Pelikan and V. Hotchkiss (eds.), *Creeds and Confessions of Faith*, vol.1 (New York and London, 2003), p. 377.
27 Florensky, "*Primechaniia sviashchennika Pavla Florenskogo*," pp. 89–175, rpt. Florensky, *Soch. v 4 tomakh*, p. 315. The commentaries were not meant for publication.
28 Ibid., pp. 308–315.
29 Ibid., p. 311.
30 Pavel Florensky, "*Ikonostas*" in his *Khristianstvo i kul'tura* (Christianity and Culture) (Moscow, 2001), p. 548; my translation.
31 Ibid., p. 545.
32 English translation from Pavel Florensky, *Iconostasis*, tr. Donald Sheelan and Olga Andrejev (Crestwood, New York, 1996, rpt. 2000), p. 65.
33 Florensky, "*Ikonostas*," p. 625; my translation.
34 In the 1920s Florensky embarked on the "*Symbolarium*" project, which was meant to develop into a dictionary of symbols. Only one issue was realized. See Elena Nekrasova, "*Neosushtestvennii zamisel 1920-h godov sozdaniia 'Symbolarium' (Slovaria simbolov) i ego pervii vipusk 'Tochka'*" (The unrealized project of the 1920s for the creation of 'Symbolarium' (Dictionary of Symbols) and its first issue 'Point" in *Pamiatniki kul'tury. Novie otkritiia* (Monuments of Culture: New Discoveries) (Annual Publication, Leningrad, 1994), pp. 99–115. The text of the first issue is on pp. 100–115.
35 Alexander Mikhailov, "O. Pavel Florensky kak filosof granitsi" (Fr. Pavel Florensky as a Philosopher of the Boundary), *Voprosi iskusstvoznaniia*, number 4, 1994.
36 Florensky, *Iconostasis*, p. 60.
37 Ibid., p. 62.
38 In Thomas Eekman and Dean S. Worth, *Russian Poetics: Proceedings of the International Colloguium at UCLA, 22–26 September 1975*, (Bloomington, Ind., 1975), pp. 393–409.
39 Sergei Khoruzhii, "The Idea of Energy in the Moscow School of Christian Neo-Platonism" in Norbert Franz, Michael Hagemeister and Frank Haney (eds.), *Pavel Florenskij – Tradition und Moderne* (Frankfurt and Berlin, 2001), pp. 73–74.
40 On the ambiguity in Palamas, especially his notion of "energy," see Bradshaw, *Aristotle East and West*, p. 273ff. On Palamas's misinterpretation of Aristotle, see Katerina Ierodiakonou, "The Anti-Logical Movement in the Fourteenth Century" in Katerina Ierodiakonou (ed.), *Byzantine Philosophy and Its Sources* (Oxford, 2002), pp. 219–237.
41 See Williams, "The Philosophical Structures of Palamism," pp. 27–44.
42 Khoruzhii, "The Idea of Energy in the Moscow School of Christian Neo-Platonism," p. 69.
43 Ibid., p. 74.
44 Pavel Florensky, "*Obshchechelovecheskie korni idealizma*" (The Universal Roots of Idealism) (1909) in his *Soch. v cheterekh tomakh*, vol.3 (Moscow, 1999), p. 151.
45 On this see Pelikan, *The Christian Tradition*, vol.2: *The Spirit of Eastern Christendom*, pp. 264–267.

46 Panayiotis Chrestou, "The Theology of Gregory Palamas" in his *An Introduction to the Study of the Church Fathers* (Rollinsford, NH, 2005), p. 190.
47 See Fadi Georgi, "The Vision of God as a Foretaste of the Eternal Life according to St. Gregory Palamas" in Martin Tamcke (ed.), *Gotteserlebnis und Gotteslehre: Christliche und islamische Mystik im Orient* (Wiesbaden, 2010), p. 148.
48 Ibid.

2 The unity of the icon in space
On a stage in man's road to deification

In the first part of this chapter, I claim that Florensky's notion of the pictorial space of the icon goes back, on one level, to his earlier interest in the construction of Cubist space. By depicting the object in its unity in space, both principles of spatial construction – in icons and in Cubist images – are interpreted by the Russian thinker as a challenge to Renaissance linear space and, more generally, the Cartesian worldview. The second part of the chapter draws the visual implications of deification (*theosis*), a theological doctrine which is central to Eastern Orthodox theology and which runs as a thread through much of the Russian religious philosophy of full unity. In the third part, I bring the main ideas of the previous two sections together by putting forward the following hypothesis: Florensky's notion of the "supplementary planes" of the icon can be understood as offering a model of man's imitation of divine "vision." Thus, the religious-visual experience before the icon can become a stage on man's road to deification.

The unity of the image in space: from Cubism to icons

On a Sunday morning in 1913, Florensky and his friend Sergei Bulgakov, two of the greatest Russian religious philosophers, went together to see the Shchukin Collection in Moscow. They were especially interested in the newly acquired Picasso paintings. The collection belonged to and was housed in the private residence of a wealthy merchant, Sergei Shchukin (1854–1936). From 1907 on, it was open to the public on Sundays. Shchukin, whose two brothers were avid collectors of icons, had an almost unerring eye for great contemporary art. He was one of the earliest patrons of Picasso, long before Picasso became an international celebrity. He knew Matisse personally, and hosted him in his mansion in 1911.[1] During his stay in Moscow, Matisse was greatly impressed by the art of the Russian icon. His enthusiasm was one of the avenues through which icons attracted the attention of the avant-garde, both inside and outside Russia.

Bulgakov and Florensky were certainly impressed by Shchukin's Picassos. In the case of Bulgakov, the reaction was strongly worded and negative.[2] Florensky was a bit more nuanced. In his book *Smisl' idealizma* (The Meaning of Idealism) (1914), Florensky analyzes Picasso's treatment of pictorial space in particular. The construction of space of early Analytical Cubism, of which Picasso's paintings in Moscow were an example, was underlined by a fundamentally different logic than that of Renaissance linear perspective. The latter represented the way an object appeared from one point of view; the former, by representing different aspects of an object, gave an idea of the object in its totality. In this sense, Cubist space was superior to linear space. Let me briefly summarize Florensky's argument.

In Cubism, according to Florensky, "the reality of the artistic image is realized in [. . .] unifying in one apperception that which is given in different moments and, consequently, under different angles of vision."[3] He cites the artist and writer Alexei Grishchenko, who had considered the same Picasso pieces: "The division of the object into parts becomes a necessary element in Picasso's paintings. [. . .] We see the represented object from several points of view."[4] In other words, Florensky refers to what present-day art historians have described as the "multiple planes" of some Cubist images, i.e. "the simultaneous representation of entirely different viewpoints, the sum total of which constitutes the object."[5] One of the best-known examples of this kind of spatial treatment of the figure is Picasso's *Les Demoiselles d'Avignon* (1907). Russian Cubo-Futurists such as Natalia Goncharova used the same principle in some of her works, as in her portrait of Mikhail Larionov, in which the "distortion" of the face is the result of the representation of different aspects of the face (in simple words, there is a mixture of profile and frontal views) alongside each other on the same picture plane (Figure 2.1).

The terms in which Florensky described Cubist space in his 1914 book sound inescapably close to the opening sections of his essay "Reverse Perspective" (written in 1919 and presented as a lecture the following year). "Reverse perspective" is the established term for describing the construction of pictorial space in the medieval icon.[6] According to Florensky, one of the fundamental features of the organization of iconic space lies in the representation of "parts and surfaces [of the same object] which cannot be seen simultaneously"[7] from a fixed position. This phenomenon is especially noticeable in treatments of relatively simple objects in icons. Let us look at two icons from Richard Temple's wonderful collection in London. In Figure 2.2, St. Mark is resting his feet on a foot-stool, the sides of which are represented from several intersecting points of view – a view from above, which allows us to see the entire top unforeshortened, as well as two side views – all of which conflict with the aspect with which the figure itself is

38 *The unity of the icon in space*

Figure 2.1 Natalia Goncharova, *Portrait of Mikhail Larionov*, 1913, Museum Ludwig, Köln/Cologne, Schenkung Sammlung Ludwig/Donation Ludwig Collection 2011; permission by Rheinisches Bildarchiv, Cologne (RBA).

represented. The depiction of the writing table follows a similar visual logic. Notice that the upper part is seen under a different angle from the lower part of the table. As a result, the sides of the table are almost parallel in one area, while they are diverging in the other. The eccentric shape of the coffin of

The unity of the icon in space 39

Figure 2.2 St. Mark the Evangelist, Russian, Tver School, sixteenth century, 55.5 × 41.5 cm., Temple Gallery, London; permission by the Temple Gallery and Richard Temple.

St. Nicholas the Miracle-Worker in Figure 2.3 can also be explained by the representation, in icon space, of aspects of the object which could not be seen at the same time. We are shown a frontal view of one side of the coffin. The other side of the coffin, which is also depicted, cannot be seen from

40 *The unity of the icon in space*

Figure 2.3 The Death of St. Nicholas, Russian, Mstera School, late nineteenth century, 31.5 × 27.0 cm., Temple Gallery, London; permission by the Temple Gallery and Richard Temple.

the standpoint from which we perceive the first side. The saint's body and the upper part of the coffin are shown from an entirely different perspective from above. The representation of these different aspects on the same picture plane can be read exactly in terms of Florensky's notion of the "supplementary planes" – i.e. the showing of aspects of the object that should not be there according to the laws of normal vision at a given moment of time. As Florensky noticed, in some cases these aspects are emphasized by means of colour. These "additional"/"supplementary" surfaces are often painted in strikingly bright colours that capture the viewer's attention.

Several ideas come up in Florensky's passages cited earlier in this chapter. Firstly, it is notable that his interest in the medieval icon was provoked by an earlier interest in contemporary avant-garde art (in this case Picasso).[8] This was not unusual and, in fact, represented the typically Russian reception of Western modernist art. For the Russians, Western avant-garde movements frequently provided the starting ground for their appreciation of their own native tradition of the icon. As Vasilii Kandinsky, one of the best-known Russian modernist artists abroad, explained, an exhibition of French Impressionism that he saw in 1895 helped him acquire "an eye for the abstract in art" and "from that moment on" he looked at "the art of icons with different eyes."[9] The connection between Western modernist art and the tradition of medieval Russian art was already realised at that time by artists and critics alike. Vladimir Markov's *Principles of the New Art* (1912) made the link between icons and modernist images explicit. The artist Alexei Grishchenko published an influential book under the revealing title *On the Connection between Russian Painting with Byzantium and the West* (1913), from which Florensky quoted in his *The Meaning of Idealism*. The affinity between avant-garde images and icons was the subject of several pieces by Nikolai Punin, one of the most perceptive art critics at the time, for example "Directions in Contemporary Art and Russian Icon-painting" (1913). Another advocate of the avant-garde, the critic Nikolai Tarabukin, was also actively engaged in the debate. His *The Meaning of Icons* (likely conceived in 1916, though published only in the 1980s) was followed by *From the Easel to the Machine* (1923), in which he compared icons as functional sacred objects to the products of industrial mass production.

Secondly, another observation needs to be made at this stage. The interest of Florensky, a religious thinker and a priest, in Picasso was by no means unique. It is a testament to the profound significance of the visual for Russian religious philosophy that Cubism provoked such passionate reactions exactly among religious intellectuals.[10] As I have been claiming throughout this book, questions of visuality that are seen in Western thought as belonging to the field of art history were an integral and natural part of a religious-philosophical discourse in early twentieth-century Russia. It should not come as a surprise that a number of these authors would turn their attention a few years later to the problem of the icon. Interestingly, none of them, including Florensky, mentions explicitly in their writings on the medieval image their earlier engagement with Western modernist art in general and Cubism in particular. At the same time, the connections are sometimes quite striking to be missed at a closer reading.

If, for instance, Florensky's two texts – *The Meaning of Idealism* (1914) and "Reverse Perspective" (1919) – are interpreted alongside each other, the obvious implication that emerges is that some of the greatest experiments of modern art – which strike us as utterly original and novel – have for centuries been part of the visual language of the icon. Further, and perhaps more importantly, the recognized common quality that the art of the icon and avant-garde art share is a drive towards anti-illusionism, which challenges the mode of image-making that has been prevalent in the West since the Renaissance (in the case of the avant-garde, this was a deliberate and conscious reaction against the art of the past). In this way, both provide a model of visuality that offered an alternative to Renaissance art and Albertian perspectivism and, ultimately, counteract the prevalent epistemological model which underlined the modern, rationalistic worldview. Simply put, both the icon and avant-garde art are interpreted in the same light, i.e. as alternatives to rationalism and positivism. Finally, whatever parallels we might draw between the icon and the avant-garde image – here, the parallel is between principles of the construction of pictorial space – their respective value is not the same. The construction of space in Cubist art presupposes a certain type of vision, what Florensky calls "synthetic vision."[11] This vision, though, is forced and artificial because it is not the result of the spiritual evolution of the individual. It is only within the Platonic-Christian worldview that "synthetic vision" becomes also "spiritual vision" that is a feature of man's power to go beyond the "fleshy" (*plotskii*) sensible world.[12]

Thus, the whole emphasis of Florensky's text moves away from the concrete instances of Cubism and goes back to the author's larger topic of idealism, specifically Platonic idealism. Florensky considers the possibility of developing a "new habit of seeing" (Plato, *Republic*, 517 E) to be a task already posed by Plato, most famously in the myth of the cave: What does it mean "to see the ideas"? His reply comes down to the notion that man has to develop his spiritual "capacity for mystical contemplation" and his ability to see Platonic Ideas "directly, face to face."[13] The images revealed to man in this process of "mystical contemplation" are defined as four-dimensional and as such possessing "a higher degree of reality."[14] This thinking, according to Florensky, lies at the basis of a "generic method of looking at the world," which is interested in the phenomenon "as a whole" and not only in "one moment of its history."[15] Modern man has lost exactly this ability to experience "the world as a unified being."[16] Thus, if art has a mission, it consists in restoring to humanity the ability to "see the wood behind the trees."[17] This is the meaning of "spiritual vision," and the principle of "supplementary planes" provides a visual expression of it.

At this stage, I would like to place Florensky's ideas on pictorial space in Cubism and in icons within the larger context of Russian religious philosophy. What Florensky does is to take a largely technical issue in the history of art – namely, the problem of perspective – and turn it into a philosophical problem which touches on many of the issues that lay at the heart of Russian religious philosophy.

"The pure in heart shall see God:" the visual language of the doctrine of deification

At the age of twenty-three, Florensky published an article titled "*Tipakh vozrastaniia*" (The Types of Human Growth), which talks about the possibility that a "person of a higher type" (*lichnost' vishego tipa*) embodies Christ.[18] This early, short text is interesting because it plays on several themes that become major in Florensky's later writings. For example, it foreshadows Florensky's ideas on religious individualism that run throughout his work and are wedded to his dissatisfaction with modern individualism, which he calls "self-deification" (*samoobozhestvleniia*). The Russian thinker's notion of the religious individual bears analogies with Ernst Troeltsch's better-known – at least, in the West – description of early Christians as "individuals-in-relation-to-God,"[19] In both cases – with Florensky and with Troeltsch – we have a notion of human freedom which is only possible given man's awareness of his connection with God. There is, however, a typically Eastern Orthodox background to this idea, which grows out of the theological doctrine of *theosis* (usually translated into English as "deification"). With Florensky, as most famously with Soloviev and Dostoevsky, the "self-deification" of modern man is always contrasted with the Eastern Orthodox view of the dignity and worth of man, who carries within himself the divine gift of *theosis*.

For the doctrine of *theosis* I will refer mainly to the most recent and authoritative study on the subject: Norman Russell's *The Doctrine of Deification in Greek Patristic Thought* (2004). I will also keep close to Vladimir Lossky's classic *The Mystical Theology of the Eastern Church* (1944) and other works.[20] As a definition of *theosis*, a term coined by Gregory Nazianzus (ca. 329–ca. 389), I will use the one by Dionysius the Areopagite (known also as Pseudo-Dionysius) (fl. ca. 500) in *The Ecclesiastical Hierarchies*: "Deification is the attaining of likeness to God and union with him so far as it is possible" (*EH* I.3 in PG 3.376A). The very possibility for deification is predicated on Christ's Incarnation. In the words of Gregory Nazianzus, "it was necessary that man should be sanctified by the humanity of God."[21] The frequently repeated formula, first used by St. Irenaus (whence it entered the Orthodox tradition), was that "God made Himself man that man might become God."[22] My primary concern in this chapter will be the visual implications of the doctrine of *theosis*. It is, therefore, worthwhile noticing that "likeness" or the Greek *homoisis* is used by Dionysius and later Byzantine theologians both in the context of man's relationship to God and in reference to the relationship between image and prototype. In other words, what is posited is a likeness between man and God, and between icon and prototype – two ideas that frequently run alongside each other.

Theosis is a doctrine typical of Eastern Orthodox theology. It is by no means accepted, especially in its Palamite interpretation,[23] by all Christians outside the Orthodox tradition of thought.[24] For the Orthodox, however, *theosis* is the central, defining feature of their faith. If there is any argument, it is not about the validity of the doctrine but about the degree of its reliance on ancient, especially Platonic, sources. It is on this issue (i.e. the relationship between Platonism and Christianity) that Florensky hit a nerve. He posited a continuity which seemed to mask major differences between the two systems of thought and which many theologians, both in the East and in the West, have found and will find disturbing. Since most scholars would agree that Platonism played a role in the evolution of Christianity – while disagreeing about the importance of this role – it is significant that Florensky adopts explicitly such a provocative view, i.e. the formula "from magic to Platonism and then to Christianity." When Florensky asked "Where does Platonism come from?" his answer is "from magic."[25] This understanding acquires a profound meaning against the frequently repeated view about "the continuity of our spiritual culture from Platonism."[26] In this sense, as long as our focus is on Florensky, we need to take seriously the pre-Christian, Platonic, and even earlier ideas on deification and their relationship to visuality.

Surely, Plato's "likeness to God as far as possible" (*Theaet.* 176b) sounds akin to Dionysius's definition. Russell seems to claim that this is a similarity mainly on the level of language. According to him, "deification has biblical roots," but it "came to be expressed in the language of Hellenism,"[27] conceding at the same time that "without Platonism there is no philosophical approach to deification."[28] While ideas of man's deification are absent in the Old Testament, it is true that the New Testament abounds with them. There is the much-cited Psalm 82:6: "I said, you are gods and all of you the son of the Most High," as well as St. Peter's description of man as "a partaker of the divine nature" (II. Peter I:4). At the same time, there is a much more ancient background, going back to pagan mystery cults and Orphism, to the notion that deification is the result of the religious development of the individual. Interestingly, the experience of the initiated in the cults is frequently described through metaphors of light and seeing the divine face to face. For instance, Apuleius of Madaura in his *Metamorphosis* (popularly known as the *Golden Ass*) has the initiated hero Lucius say at the climax of the rites of the mystery of Isis that he "saw the sun flashing with bright effulgence" and "approached close to the gods above and the gods below and worshipped them face to face."²⁹ After the rites, Apuleius tells us, Lucius was presented to the crowd in the guise of Osiris, thus being identified with the god. As Russell notes, the strongly negative stand of early Christian authors on pagan mysteries did not prevent them from using a language reminiscent of the descriptions of the experiences of the initiates of the mystery cults.³⁰

Plato's idea of the vision of blessedness which can be attained only once the soul has freed itself from the prison of the body (*Phaedo* 81a and *Phaedr.* 250b), too, goes back to Orphism and its conception of the dual nature of man.³¹ While the contrast between body and soul is, in many important ways, foreign to the spirit of Eastern Orthodoxy and even more so to the Russian concept of full unity, Plato's notion that the soul's ability to apprehend Ideas makes it akin to the divine (*Phaedo* 82e) would have a long life in the Eastern Church. "Apprehending Ideas," "seeing the sun," "worshipping the gods face to face" in pagan Platonism are all metaphors that play on visuality but suggest an experience beyond the visual. This is very much the case in Christian theology as well, which takes seriously Jesus's promise: "Blessed are the pure in heart for they shall see God" (Matthew 5–8). There is a clear implication running through the entire Platonic-Christian corpus on deification, that the "vision" of the One or of God is a gift to the "pure in heart" – i.e. those who have gone through a process of purification. This process, which the ancient Greeks called *catharsis*, is exactly what Florensky meant by transcending "the fleshy" (see the previous section, "The unity of the image in space," especially p.42). There is another idea, though, which never becomes quite explicit in the literature on *theosis*, but always lurks behind, namely that an aspect of the process of purification involves the evolution of human vision. At a certain stage in this process, a kind of vision is developed which holds an intermediary position between natural vision and the state beyond vision. It is this idea, hinted at by pagan philosophers and medieval theologians, that Florensky engages with; this is where, I believe, his contribution to the doctrine of *theosis* lies.

There are several questions that naturally arise even after such a brief survey of the literature on *theosis* as the one here. Most obviously, why does a doctrine of man's transcendence of his humanity, which implies transcending the human senses – including, of course, the sense of vision – consistently express itself through metaphors centred on human vision? Is this just a matter of language, as we are frequently told by scholars, who appear to want to excuse Christian authors for using the language of visuality that ultimately derives from pagan, especially Platonic philosophy? Or is there a deeper reason that visual concepts became the appropriate vehicle for the expression of the theological doctrine under our attention? Further, why is union with the One, with the Neo-Platonists, or with God, with Christian writers, described exactly as vision, having in mind that vision implies a duality between viewer and viewed? After all, the aim of *theosis* is the disappearance of such a duality at the moment of unity between man and God. This was a point that Plotinus, ever aware of the inadequacies of language, had already made (*Enn.* III 9.10–11–13; VI 9.11–4–7).

Florensky's view that the experience of "spiritual vision," afforded by the icon, marks a stage in the spiritual and religious development of a person who has transcended the "fleshy," associates him with a long line of Christian, as well as Platonic, thought playing on the notion of purification. Already the Early Christian Fathers, as Clement of Alexandria (ca. 150–ca. 215), spoke of the path to God which could be walked only by those "who have detached themselves as far as possible from everything human" (*Strom.* 2.125.5). The need for man to go beyond his corporeal state is recurrent with Pseudo-Dionysius as well: he describes "the completely divine man" as one who "will not perform what belongs to the flesh except the things which are the most necessary in accordance with nature" (*EH* 3.3.7, 433 BC). Maximus the Confessor's (580–662) notion of Christians as "emptying themselves of the passions" (*Or. Dom* 2, 877A) should be understood along the same lines. How does one transcend the "fleshy" and achieve *theosis*? The simple answer is through divine grace. Maximus expressed a well-established idea when he said that "by nature we do not have the capacity to attain deification" (*Thail.* 22, school.5, CCSG7.145.28–30) and that it was "supernatural power that brings deification" (*Opusc.* I in PG 91.33A-36A). This is where we see the role played by visual images. God manifests Himself through material, perceptible objects as a concession to our state. These material things – the icon is one example – are, as Dionysius the Areopagite wrote, "sacred veils" through which God is known. The end is, however, to attain a stage beyond the material and visual, a "truly mysterious darkness of unknowing" (MT I.3, 1000D-1001A).[32]

Two things become clear at this stage. The very precondition of becoming "gods by grace" is faith. This idea runs through the whole Eastern Orthodox tradition, and the focus on faith is very prominent with Florensky as well. Further, faith transforms man in such a way as to open the possibility of imitating God. The concept of imitation, which is already central with the Cappadocians,[33] goes to the very heart of the doctrine of *theosis*. Frequently, man's imitation of God is conceptualized in visual terms. The leitmotif of Pseudo-Dionysius's corpus, especially of his *Mystical Theology*, of the progression from purification to illumination underlies, in many ways, the whole tradition of thought I am referring to here and forms the background of Florensky's writings on the icon.

Man's imitation of divine vision as a stage to deification

In this part of the present chapter, I will draw on and further develop some of Florensky's ideas. More concretely, I will propose that his notion of the "supplementary planes" of the icon can be understood as a concrete model of man's imitation of God's "vision." According to the present interpretation, this principle of the construction of pictorial space provides a stage on man's road to deification. Imitating divine "vision" is a way of imitating God. My thesis here builds on earlier work, which I will briefly summarize.

In my book, *Space, Time, and Presence in the Icon: Seeing the World with the Eyes of God*,[34] I propose that a structural analogy could be drawn between the artistic principle of the "supplementary planes" of the icon and the Christian dogma of a timelessly eternal, simultaneously existing God. To a being who transcends the temporal dimension, events of human history exist simultaneously, all at once. By implication, such a timeless being will not perceive objects successively in time but simultaneously. In this sense, divine vision is simultaneous and thus "viewpoint-less," i.e., things are not seen from a certain point of view but, potentially, from all possible viewpoints at once. In other words, in divine vision, objects would not appear from a single point of view; all sides of an object would be perceived at the same time. While in practice, what Florensky called the "supplementary planes" of the icon never show *all* aspects of an object, they do show aspects that cannot be seen from a fixed position at one moment of time (see Figures 2.2 and 2.3). As God is not subject to spatial location, He is also ubiquitous. Very appropriately, John of Damascus writes of God's "divine, all-seeing and immaterial eye."[35] In other words, God transcends not only time but space as well, and His spacelessness becomes a metaphor for His timelessness (even though it does not literally illustrate timelessness).[36]

I would now like to build on the previous idea. I will propose that "reverse perspective," understood in Florensky's sense of "supplementary planes," suggests a mode of vision that is a stage on man's road to *theosis* (i.e. deification). In other words, by inviting us to imitate God's "vision," the pictorial space of the icon brings us one step closer in the process of our deification. So long as in Eastern Orthodox theology *theosis* is the end goal of humanity, the icon, specifically through the principle of constructing pictorial space, acquires a profound theological meaning. It is in the context of the Eastern Orthodox discourse on *theosis* that we should understand the otherwise enigmatic critical remarks by Florensky on Cubist space and "synthetic vision." As we have seen, the Russian author described Cubist pictorial space in very similar terms to the ones he used in his definition of space in the icon. At the same time, there is a fundamental difference, as it is only iconography that can be understood as a stage in the spiritual development of the individual or, in the terms I suggest here, as an aspect of *theosis*.

There is a specifically Russian intellectual background to these ideas. The doctrine of *theosis*, especially in its ethical implications, had an interesting after-life in nineteenth and early twentieth century Russia, particularly among figures associated with full unity.[37] The emphasis frequently fell on the notion of *podvig*, i.e. the courage of man to battle with everything opposed to deification, the constant struggle to conform to the image of God. While Soloviev's concept of "Godmanhood" (*bogochelovechestvo*) departs from the Orthodox doctrine in many ways, it was developed with this doctrine as its background.[38] Soloviev, in contrast, exerted an important influence on Dostoevsky,[39] whose novels, it could be claimed, cannot be fully understood without the idea of "Godmanhood." Soloviev clearly saw "Godmanhood" and the way it was embraced by Dostoevsky as part of Christian doctrine, as when he says that "inner moral rebirth" was an ideal "not invented by Dostoevsky, but bequeathed to all mankind by the Gospels."[40]

Once again, what comes across in the Russian tradition of thought on *theosis* is the consistent recourse to a language playing on visuality. Consider, for example, the commonly used Russian word (which exists in other Slavic languages as well) *bezobrazie*, which is usually translated as "outrage." *Bezobrazie*, however, literally means "without (*bez*) image (*obraz*)." In this way, with Dostoevsky, Soloviev, and others, evil is often understood as the absence of Christ's image in man.[41] In a recent and intriguing study on Dostoevsky, Rowan Williams has convincingly suggested the Russian novelist's characters can be viewed as the "iconic person" versus the "demonic person." The "iconic person" is one "whose life is shaped by what the icon represents,"[42] while the "demonic" type is "impervious to this framework."[43]

Conclusion and implications

The present chapter looked at Florensky's notion of the "supplementary planes" of the icon. It began by suggesting that the Russian thinker's idea, put forward in the classic essay "Reverse Perspective" written in 1919, was indebted to his earlier analysis in his *The Meaning of Idealism* of 1914 of a principle of the construction of space in Picasso's early works. Further, it clamed that the notion of "supplementary planes" can be developed in a theologically meaningful way as a stage on man's road to deification. It showed that the doctrine of deification (*theosis*) had a long history of being conceptualized through a language that plays on visuality. In this way, Florensky's writings on pictorial space in the icon are understood against the background of the corpus of writing on *theosis* in Eastern Orthodox theology and Russian religious philosophy.

What needs to be remembered is that the notion of "supplementary planes" is an aspect of Florensky's theory of "reverse perspective." The term "reverse perspective" seems to imply that we are dealing with an art historical issue. Indeed, "perspective," when used with respect to painting, belongs to the classical vocabulary of the discipline of the history of art. What Florensky does is take this art historical term and use it towards his larger religious-philosophical project. In fact, what he is talking about is neither "reverse" nor "perspective,"[44] but this does not matter in view of his overall aim.

So, what is Florensky's aim? As it was mentioned, the reason that the Russian thinker became interested in the problem of pictorial space in icons and Cubist images was that in both cases we are dealing with a visual model of the object in its unity in space. This visual model was clearly different from the one-point construction of linear Renaissance space. Still further, the latter was embedded in a Western, Cartesian worldview, which was the object of Florensky's criticism in particular as well as of the movement of full unity in general. However, it is only the medieval icon – not the Cubist image – that could offer a viable alternative, as it was a feature of what Florensky called the Platonic-Christian worldview. In other words, on its own, the visual image is of no value. Once it becomes the expression of a larger religious philosophical construct – in this case, the project of full unity at the heart of the Platonic-Christian worldview – it acquires the value of this construct. When one considers the literature on *theosis*, one realizes that this is a profoundly Eastern Orthodox understanding of visuality.

Notes

1 Yuri Rusakov and John Bowlt, "Matisse in Russia in the Autumn of 1911," *The Burlington Magazine*, vol.117/866, 1975, pp. 284–291.
2 Sergei Bulgakov, "*Trup krasoty*" (The Corpse of Beauty), *Russkaia misl'*, vol.8, 1915, pp. 91–106.
3 Pavel Florensky, *Smisl' idealizma* (The Meaning of Idealism) (1914) in his *Sochineniia v chetirekh tomakh* (Works in Four Volumes), vol.3 (Moscow, 1999), p. 98.
4 Ibid., p. 102.
5 Arthur Miller, *Einstein, Picasso: Space, Time, and the Beauty That Causes Havoc* (New York, 2001), p. 106.
6 On the definitions of "reverse perspective" both in Russia and in the West, see my "On the Problem of 'Reverse Perspective'," pp. 464–470.
7 Pavel Florensky, "Reverse Perspective" (written in 1919, presented as a lecture in 1920) in Pavel Florensky, *Beyond Vision: Essays on the Perception of Art*, intro. Nicoletta Misler, tr. Wendy Salmond (London, 2002), p. 201.

50 *The unity of the icon in space*

8 On the artistic evolution of the Russian avant-garde from an engagement with Western art to a deeper engagement with the icon, see my "The Icon and the Visual Arts at the Time of the Russian Religious Renaissance" in George Pattison, Caryl Emerson and Randall Poole (eds.), *The Oxford Handbook of Russian Religious Thought* (Oxford and New York, 2019), forthcoming. On the reception of Picasso in Russia, see Felix Philipp Ingold (ed.), *Picasso in Russland* (Zurich, 1973).
9 Anette Vezin and Luc Vezin, *Kandinsky and der Blaue Reiter* (Paris, 1992), p. 37.
10 Florensky and Bulgakov, as we saw; see also Nikolai Berdyaev, arguably the best-known Russian religious philosopher abroad (Nikolai Berdyaev, "Pikasso," *Sofiia*, 1914, pp. 57–62).
11 Florensky's concept of "synthetic vision" is indebted to Theosophical notions of visuality, such as the idea of "astral vision." I have paid some detailed attention to this in my "Visuality among Cubism, Iconography, and Theosophy: Pavel Florensky's Theory of the Icon," *Journal of Icon Studies*, vol.1, 2012, available online.
12 Florensky, *Smisl' idealizma* (The Meaning of Idealism), p. 114; my translation.
13 Ibid., p. 13.
14 Ibid., p. 108.
15 Ibid., p. 110.
16 Ibid., p. 108.
17 Ibid., p. 115.
18 Pavel Florensky, "*O tipakh vozrastaniia*" (The Types of Human Growth) (1906), *Bogoslovskii vestnik*, vol.7, 1906, pp. 1–39; rpt. in Pavel Florensky, *Sochineniia v cheterekh tomakh* (Works in Four Volumes) (Moscow, 1994).
19 Ernst Troeltsch, *The Social Teaching of the Christian Churches*, vols.1–2 (London, 1912, rpt. 1931; New York, 1960).
20 For example, Lossky's lectures of 1945–1946 in *The Vision of God* (Clayton, WI, 1963); also, his *In the Image and Likeness of God* (Crestwood, New York, 1974).
21 Cited in Lossky, *In the Image and Likeness of God*, p. 102.
22 See, ibid., p. 97. Lossky's comment is useful: "An ineffable descent of God to the ultimate limit of our fallen condition, even unto death – a descent of God which opens to men a path of ascent, the unlimited vistas of union of created being with Divinity."
23 On the theology of St. Gregory Palamas, see Chapter 1 here.
24 For example, Benjamin Drewery in his book on Origen expresses the concerns of many non-Orthodox theologians when he says:

> I must put it on record that deification is, in my view, the most serious aberration to be found not only in Origen but in the whole tradition to which he contributed. [. . .] My conviction [is] that here lies the disastrous flaw in Greek Christian thought.
> (Benjamin Drewery, *Origen and the Doctrine of Grace* (London, 1960), pp. 200–201)

25 Florensky, *Smisl' idealizma* (The Meaning of Idealism), p. 147; my translation. On the problem of Florensky's understanding of magic, see Leonid I. Vasilenko, "*O magii i okkul'tizme v nasledii Pavla Florenskogo*" (On Magic and Occultism in the Heritage of Pavel Florensky), *Vestnik Sviato-Tikhonovskogo Gumanitarnogo uniersiteta*, vol.3, 2004, pp. 81–99.
26 Lecture of 17 September 1908 at the Theological Academy in Moscow. Cited ibid., p. 145; my translation.

27 Norman Russell, *The Doctrine of Deification in Greek Patristic Thought* (Oxford, 2004), p. 8.
28 Ibid., p. 15.
29 Apuleius of Madaura, *Apuleius of Madauros: The Isis Book*, tr. J.G. Griffiths (Leiden, 1975), Chapter 24. On this, see Hugh Bowden, *Mystery Cults in the Ancient World* (London, 2010), Chapter "Isis," pp. 156–181.
30 Russell, *The Doctrine of Deification*, p. 32. In a similar vein, Hugh Bowden also observes the "shared vocabulary" on the background of the "little contact between Christianity and the mystery cults" (Hugh Bowden, *Mystery Cults in the Ancient World* (London, 2010), p. 207). There are scholars, however, who go in the other direction and claim that early Christianity was no more than an example of a mystery cult (Harvey Whitehouse and Luther H. Martin (eds.), *Theorizing the Religious Past: Archaeology, History, and Cognition* (Walnut Creek, 2004).
31 See Ivan Linforth, *The Arts of Orpheus* (Berkeley and Los Angeles, 1941).
32 The English translation is from *Pseudo-Dionysius: The Complete Works*, tr. Colm Luibheid (New York, 1987), p. 137. On the theme of visuality in Dionysius, see Filip Ivanovic, "Union with and Likeness to God: Deification According to Dionysius the Areopagite" in Mark Edwards and Elena Ene D-Vasilescu (eds.), *Visions of God and Ideas of Deification in Patristic Thought* (London and New York, 2017), especially section "Deification and Its Visual Aspect," pp. 143ff; by the same author, "Images of Invisible Beauty in the Aesthetic Cosmology of Dionysius the Areopagite" in Jelena Bogdanovic (ed.), *Perceptions of the Body and Sacred Space in Late Antiquity and Byzantium* (London and New York, 2018), pp. 11–23.
33 Norman Russell, "The Cappadocian Approach" in his *The Doctrine of Deification*, pp. 206–235.
34 Antonova, *Space, Time, and Presence in the Icon*.
35 John of Damascus, "The Orthodox Faith" in *Writings, Fathers of the Church*, vol.37, tr. F. Chase Jr. (Washington, 1958), p. 204.
36 Space and time in this pre-Einstein context are not to be conflated automatically. They are distinct dimensions, which are considered together through their shared transcendence in God's world.
37 For an excellent overview, see Ruth Coates, "Theosis in Early Twentieth-Century Russian Thought" in George Pattison, Caryl Emerson and Randall Poole (eds.), *The Oxford Handbook of Russian Religious Thought* (forthcoming in 2019). See also Coates' forthcoming *Deification in Russian Religious Thought: Between the Revolutions, 1905–1917* (Oxford and New York, 2019).
38 See Stephen Finlan's chapter on Soloviev in Stephen Finlan and Vladimir Kharlamov (eds.), *Theosis: Deification in Christian Theology* (Princeton, 2006); also the classic essay by Nicholai Berdyaev, "The Idea of Godmanhood in Vladimir Soloviev," *Perezvon*, number 7–8, 1925, pp. 180–182, in which the author draws attention to the idea that the concept refers to the transfiguration of the world at large rather than to individual salvation.
39 See Marina Kostalevsky, *Dostoevsky and Soloviev: The Art of Integral Vision* (New Haven and London, 1997), esp. pp. 81ff.
40 Cited ibid., p. 26.
41 Kostalevsky, *Dostoevsky and Soloviev*, p. 148.
42 Williams, *Dostoevsky*, p. 197.
43 Ibid., p. 201.
44 On this, see Kemp and Antonova, "'Reverse Perspective'," pp. 399–433.

3 The unity of faith and reason
On an unusual application of Non-Euclidean geometry

In this chapter, I consider Florensky's take on one of the most persistent themes in the Russian philosophy of full unity, namely the unity of faith and reason, religion and science. The unity of faith and reason was ultimately meant to counteract what the Russians saw as the problem-ridden disjunction between religious and secular thought in much of Western philosophy. In the first section I look at Florensky's explicit aim of developing a "mathematical worldview," one which applied mathematics to an understanding of the world which was fundamentally religious-philosophical and which challenged the one-sidedness of the Western "analytical worldview." In the second section I draw attention to one specific example of the phenomenon of building bridges between scientific and non-scientific contexts, namely the applications of the theme of Non-Euclidean geometry in Russian intellectual history at the beginning of the twentieth century. While Non-Euclidean geometry played an important role in Western culture at that time, there is a typically Russian, Dostoevskian interpretation which draws a link between the scientific theory of Non-Euclidean geometry and the problem of religion in modernity.

In the third section, I consider a little-remarked elaboration of the Dostoevskian theme in Florensky's critique of the medieval icon. It was Florensky who first introduced the notion that iconic space (i.e. the so-called reverse perspective) is curved in a manner similar to that of the curved space of Non-Euclidean geometry.[1] His highly original use of the trope of Non-Euclidean geometry is part of a Russian religious-philosophical tradition of using a scientific theory in a loose sense in non-scientific contexts, in which this theory advanced larger philosophical projects.

Florensky and the development of a mathematical worldview

In the early 1920s, the participants in the Eighth Electro-Technical Conference in Moscow were treated to an unusual sight: a man, dressed in a

The unity of faith and reason 53

priestly cassock, walked to the platform to present some of the most recent research that was being done in the field of electricity. The man was Florensky and he held one of the highest positions in the Glavelektro, the State Commission for the Electrification of Russia, which had been initiated by Lenin. Leon Trotsky, one of the leading and most powerful Bolsheviks at the time, saw Florensky and felt bound to give him some fashion advice along the lines of a two-piece suit and some trimming of the hair and beard. Apparently, the recommendation was not followed as we see photographs of Florensky sitting in the front row of scientific conferences, still in the same priestly attire.

For Florensky, the role of a priest-scientist was completely natural. In the spirit of full unity, he was deeply committed to the view that the very antinomy between faith and reason, theology and science was artificial, wrong, and even dangerous. Faith and reason, as Florensky wrote, were "equally necessary to man, equally valuable and sacred. [. . .] One sacred matter (*odna sviatost'*) [cannot] 'contradict' the other."[2] Contemporary scholars have maintained, with a great degree of truth, that "without understanding the significance of mathematics in his [Florensky's] method of knowing the world [. . .] [it is] impossible to adequately assess his method and his philosophical views."[3]

So what is the significance of mathematics in Florensky's work? Can we describe Florensky as a mathematician? If so, what are his contributions to the field of pure mathematics? It is revealing that the great Russian mathematician Nikolai Luzin (1882–1950), a close friend of Florensky's who was left in a state of awe by his philosophical writings,[4] considered his mathematical work "worthless."[5] Indeed, if one reads Florensky's *Mnimosti v geometrii* (Imaginaries in Geometry) (1922) as a science tract, one would be confused, if not put off, by the promotion of a Ptolomeic view of the cosmos alongside attacks on the Copernican system. This is not the kind of science that most people would want taught to their children. At the same time, just as I have insisted that Florensky's work should not be understood simply as a contribution to the field of art history as such, I believe that none of it should be read as a treatise in pure science (his projects on applied science belong to a different category). Florensky's writings are valuable as comprising a religious philosophy which subjected all the material that the author was dealing with – including from art history and science – to serve his overall religious project. In this sense, the frequent attempts by Florensky's admirers to demonstrate his genius in mathematics and other fields are, in my view, based on a misunderstanding of Florensky's purpose.

There is a sense in which Ernst Kolman (1892–1979), a Czech Marxist who spent much of his time in Soviet Russia denouncing "bourgeois scientists" to the Stalinist regime, captured something of the nature of Florensky's project. Kolman referred to Florensky as one of the group of "diplomaed lackeys of priestcraft [who] right under our noses are using mathematics for a highly masked form of religious propaganda."[6] What Kolman called "religious propaganda" is what I refer to as a "religious project of modernity" in the tradition of Russian full unity – and there was nothing "masked" about it, as the idea of a "mathematical worldview" in the service of religious understanding of the world is one of the most persistent themes in Florensky's oeuvre. Already as a young man he had explained, in a letter to his mother, that to him mathematics was "a key to a worldview." Within such a worldview, "religion is given a completely new meaning."[7] This is why we should take seriously the claim of the contemporary Russian scholar Sergei Demidov that to understand Florensky's religious philosophy we should take account of Florensky's commitment to what he himself called "a mathematical worldview."[8]

The notion of a "mathematical worldview" goes back to the Russian mathematician Nikolai Bugaev (1837–1903). Florensky, a close friend of Bugaev's son, the Symbolist poet Andrei Bely, saw himself as a follower of Bugaev. Bugaev was important for Florensky as he had addressed one of the main problems that the full unity movement had identified, namely the fragmentariness of the mainstream of Western culture. Bugaev's idea was that the "mathematical worldview" was unified, as it took account of the different aspects of reality, and therefore, it challenged the one-sidedness of the "analytical worldview" (understand "that of Western philosophy").[9] In simple words, a "mathematical worldview" is not about mathematics per se; it is about utilizing mathematics in the study of a multifaceted, yet unified, reality.

It is revealing that in his essay, "*O simvolakh bezkonechnogo*" (On the Symbols of Infinity) (1904), Florensky coupled Bugaev with the German mathematician Georg Cantor (1845–1918). Much of the work of the Moscow School of Mathematics, led by Bugaev's star student Egorov and by Luzin, was, in fact, taken as a further elaboration of Cantor's set theory. It is only natural, given Florensky's intellectual orientation and his affiliation to the Moscow School, that he should be drawn to Cantor. The notion of a "set" (*die Menge* in German) was put into circulation by the Czech priest and mathematician Bernard Bolzano (1781–1848), and it was meant to explain his concept of "actual infinity." A "set" is a collection of objects that share some property. There are sets with a finite number of elements and ones with an infinite number. In his set theory, Cantor explicitly defined a "set" in Platonic terms, as a "Platonic *eidos* or idea." The idea that captured Florensky's imagination was also fundamentally Platonic and it had to do with the naming of sets in set theory. A set became real by being named in a similar way that the Name-Worshippers had claimed that God became real by being named (see Chapter 1 on the Name-Worshipping

The unity of faith and reason 55

controversy). Florensky even ventured to propose that "the set of all sets" might be God.[10]

In this chapter, I draw attention to a much less known aspect of Florensky's application of scientific ideas to his philosophy, namely his recourse to Non-Euclidean geometry as a way of explaining the construction of pictorial space in the icon. What I would like to point out at the very beginning is that the question: "Is Florensky's claim that the pictorial space of the medieval image is Non-Euclidean scientifically defensible?" is misplaced. The short answer would be no,[11] but that would miss the point. Florensky's use of Non-Euclidean geometry should be understood, in my view, not as a scientific proposition, but as an illustration of a "mathematical worldview" which brings faith and reason in a unified whole.

Non-Euclidean geometry in Russia: the non-scientific contexts of a scientific theory

The Russian contribution to the history of Non-Euclidean geometry is well known. The first system of Non-Euclidean geometry was worked out at the beginning of the nineteenth century by Nikolai Ivanovich Lobachevsky (1792–1856), a professor at the University of Kazan in Russia, independently of the Hungarian Janos Bolyai (1802–1860). A second variant was proposed later in the century by the German mathematician Bernhard Riemann (1826–1866).[12] In Russia, as well as in the West,[13] Non-Euclidean geometry exercised a huge fascination in fields well beyond the hard sciences – in philosophy, poetry, the visual arts, etc. It is notable, though, that in all these contexts Non-Euclidean geometry was used in a loose sense, which served larger philosophical arguments. For the purposes of philosophers, artists, etc., the scientific validity of their statements appeared to be of little interest. In Russian philosophical circles in particular, the vogue for Non-Euclidean geometry was very much due to the fact that it was seen as refuting the modern, Kantian worldview.[14]

Let us go back to the two variants of Non-Euclidean geometry. Both the geometry of Lobachevsky and Bolyai and that of Riemann arose from attempts (which had gone on for two millennia) to prove Euclid's Fifth Postulate. The implication of Euclid's Postulate seemed obvious, but turned out to be impossible to prove.[15] In simple words, according to Euclid, through a point that is not lying on a given line no more than one line can be drawn that is parallel to the given line. According to Lobachevsky and Bolyai, there were at least two such lines going through a point and parallel to the given line, while in Riemann's variant, there are no parallel lines at all. Riemann's geometry is just as counter-intuitive as Lobachevsky's and Bolyai's, but it is easier to visualize. This is probably why Florensky's references would be exclusively to Riemann. To visualize Riemann's variant of Non-Euclidean geometry, one just needs to imagine doing geometry on a sphere instead of a plane – something that mapmakers do all the time.[16] On a sphere, a line l would pass through both the South and the North poles. A line passing through Point P, which is off of Line l, would intersect Line l at the poles (Figure 3.1). Thus, the latter line could not be parallel to Line l.

In 1893, on occasion of the centennial celebration of Lobachevsky's birth, translations into Russian of works by Riemann, Hermann von Helmholtz (who was largely responsible for popularizing Non-Euclidean geometry to a non-professional audience), and others became available. A.V. Vasiliev of the University of Kazan edited a book, titled *Noviie idei v matematike* (New Ideas in Mathematics) (1913), which included a number of texts relating to the subject. The interest of some prominent figures of the Russian avant-garde in Non-Euclidean geometry in the 1920s should be understood to some degree at least within this context. Another graduate in mathematics at Kazan and one of the foremost Futurist poets, Velimir Khlebnikov, revealed a persistent interest in Non-Euclidean geometry – which for him, as for others, became a symbol of freedom. In a poem dedicated to the Cossack rebel Stepan Razin, Khlebnikov refers to himself as "a Razin with the banner of Lobachevsky."[17] The avant-garde painters El Lissitzky as well as Matyushin revealed in their art and their writings a concern with curved space, and with them, too, the notion of freedom is essential. The case of Khlebnikov is interesting, because for someone who was familiar with the

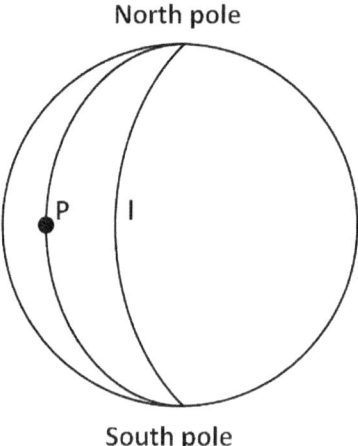

Figure 3.1 Geometry on a sphere, illustrating Riemann's variant of Non-Euclidean geometry; drawing and permission by Marian Kovacik.

mathematical and scientific side of the question, he intentionally chose to turn Non-Euclidean geometry into a metaphor.

It is easy to see why the avant-garde in Russia in the 1920s and elsewhere was drawn to the idea of curved space. In artistic terms, curved space challenged the very premises on which the construction of linear perspective was built, and modernist art was underlined by a passionate revolt against standard perspective. In philosophical terms, it challenged Kant's philosophy which postulated that the axioms of geometry were *a priori* (i.e. could not be known by experience) and were inherent to us. The very possibility of imagining other geometries put this position in question and, by implication, undermined the modern, Kantian worldview. The anti-Kantian stance was an integral aspect of the Russian philosophy of full unity and a recurrent theme with practically each member of the group.

Florensky would refer to Non-Euclidean geometry in a similarly loose fashion. According to the interpretation suggested here, Florensky's approach was close to the spirit of Dostoevsky, since he used Non-Euclidean geometry as a means of problematizing and going to the heart of a profoundly Christian worldview.[18] In Dostoevsky's *The Brothers Karamazov* (1880), one of the characters, Ivan Karamazov, having refused to accept God on God's terms, brought up the topic:

> If God really exists and if he really has created the world, then, as we all know, he created it in accordance with Euclidean geometry, and he created the human mind with the conception of only three dimensions of space. And yet there have been and there still are mathematicians and philosophers, who doubt whether the whole universe [. . .] was created only according to Euclidean geometry and they even dare to dream that two parallel lines which, according to Euclid, can never meet on earth, may meet somewhere in infinity. I, my dear chap, have come to the conclusion that if I can't understand even that, then how can I be expected to understand about God?[19]

For Florensky, drawing a link between Non-Euclidean geometry and iconic space was much more than an intriguing notion, as it ultimately came down to the implied claim that the icon in its embeddedness in a religious worldview could offer a viable counter-model of visuality to the one that had been dominant since the Renaissance and especially the Enlightenment. In the process, Florensky turned around Ivan Karamazov's idea that if God exists, He created the world "in accordance with Euclidean geometry." By taking account of developments in modern science and geometry, Florensky's point, as we will see, is that "space as we perceive it" has a "Non-Euclidean character"[20] and the icon gives instances of it.

Florensky popularized his ideas on the topic in his lecture "Reverse Perspective," given in 1920 at the Moscow Institute of Historical and Artistic Researches and Museology. In his talk the Russian thinker drew attention to a persistent characteristic of space in the icon and namely the frequent representation of straight lines as curved. This treatment of lines, according to Florensky, gives rise to a general curvature of iconic space, which bears analogies to the curved space of Non-Euclidean geometry. This hypothesis is set against the contrast that Florensky draws between Euclidean and Non-Euclidean space, where the latter is interpreted as offering a counter-model to the former, which supports a modern, secular, Kantian worldview.

The impact of Florensky's lecture must have been significant, because ideas from this short text circulated at the time and later. For example, there is a manuscript – "*Filosofiia ikony*" (The Philosophy of the Icon) (c.1922–1923), by Nikolai Tarabukin, a member of the Moscow institute – which draws an explicit connection between the pictorial construction of space in the icon and Non-Euclidean geometry. In a relevant paragraph, Tarabukin writes:

> The icon-painter thinks in a non-Euclidean way. He rejects perspective as a form of expressing infinite space. The world of icon-painting is finite. [. . .] Space in icon-painting is limited and dynamic. [. . .] I don't claim that this is the space of Riemann or Lobachevsky, incorporated in artistic form and visually formulated many centuries before them. But that this space is spherical (and not flat) and, as such, finite in one sense or another, is, beyond doubt, in all its visible features.[21]

What is interesting is that the very connection between the pictorial space in the icon and Non-Euclidean geometry became, first via Florensky, a well-established topic in Russian critiques of the icon in the 1920s. It is revealing of a typically Russian reception of Non-Euclidean ideas, whereby a scientific theory was taken up and turned into a metaphor. The appropriateness of the application of the nineteenth century notion of Non-Euclidean geometry to a medieval artistic practice is, of course, questionable. At the same time, what Florensky and his followers did was to turn a popular scientific idea into an effective metaphor, advancing their own religious-philosophical project.

The curved space of icons

Elsewhere, I outlined six different definitions of the term "reverse perspective" (some of them contradictory) that run through Florensky's essay on the topic.[22] The analogy with Non-Euclidean geometry refers to one of these definitions[23] and it is probably the least well-known among Western scholars. The idea is promising because it demonstrates that the space of the icon is highly complex and fundamentally different from that of linear space. There is still a great deal of misunderstanding about the nature of the pictorial space of the icon, as the term "reverse perspective" seems to suggest that what happens is a turning around of the laws of standard Renaissance perspective. As I have suggested in a joint paper with Martin Kemp, this is surely a historical fallacy, as "reverse perspective" had existed for centuries before the invention of linear pictorial space.[24] In this sense, it is ironic that Florensky's first reference to Non-Euclidean geometry should occur in the context of the otherwise profitless discussion on "reverse perspective" as turning around the rules of linear pictorial space. It is in the context of the opposition between "reverse" and linear perspective that Euclid is mentioned.

Florensky outlines six preconditions for linear perspective, which he holds to be false, an opinion justified by scientific research in the nineteenth century, especially in Germany and Austria. "Reverse perspective" does not subscribe to these preconditions and is thus defined in terms of their negation. My concern is with the first and basic premise, from which all others proceed – that of Euclidean space. Linear perspective is based on the notion that we live in an Euclidean three-dimensional space (a belief shared by Ivan Karamazov) of which our vision gives us instances and to which instances pictorial perspective gives a permanent visual form. However, as Florensky points out, citing Ernst Mach, there are three levels that need to be distinguished in the problem of space, of which abstract, geometrical space is only a particular case. At the level of physical space there is no reason to say that it is Euclidean.[25] Physiological space is not Euclidean either, and, according to Mach: "If we accept that physiological space is innate to us, it displays too few resemblances to geometrical space to allow us to see in it sufficient basis for a developed *a priori* geometry (in the Kantian sense)."[26] Further:

> Geometrical space is of the same nature everywhere and in all directions; it is boundless and, in Riemann's sense, infinite. Visual space is bounded and finite and what is more its extension is different in different directions, as a glance at the flattened "vault of heaven" teaches us.[27]

As was mentioned, the premises of linear perspective do not apply in the case of reverse perspective. The space in the icon *does not* follow Euclidean laws. The implied claim – clearly stated in other texts[28] – is that the pictorial space of the icon gives us visual instances of Non-Euclidean geometry.

Florensky provided hardly any concrete visual analysis of his largely theoretical positions. If we want to see how the curvature of iconic space works in visual terms we have to turn elsewhere. Lev Zhegin, an artist and a friend of Florensky's, offers in his book *Iazik zhivopisnogo proizvedeniia* (The Language of the Work of Art) (1970), the most comprehensive commentary on ideas which in the main derive from Florensky, with a wealth of visual material. Above all, he seems to have realized the importance of Florensky's fragmentary references to Non-Euclidean geometry and he consistently uses the term "system of concavity" (*sistema vognutosti*) as a synonym of "reverse perspective," which is "different from the system of Euclid."[29] It is notable that Zhegin, just like Tarabukin earlier, avoids making the explicit claim that the space of the icon is Non-Euclidean. In other words, he too understands the Non-Euclidean theme largely out of its scientific connotation. In the "system of concavity," according to Zhegin, the line of the horizon becomes arched, while the objects and figures bend (*vigibaetsia*). This phenomenon is at the heart of many "deformations" from the point of view of standard perspective of shapes and forms in "reverse perspective." Rectangular forms are frequently treated as if drawn on a concave surface. This is especially clear with simple geometrical forms, as, for instance the building in a fresco from Kahriye Camii, Constantinople (Figure 3.2). While the structure on the right still retains its rectangular shape, the one on the left has a highly unusual curved shape, which can be interpreted as the result of the bending of the originally rectangular form on a concave surface (the inner side of a sphere) (Figure 3.3).

One of the most characteristic forms of "reverse perspective," according to Zhegin, is the "barrel-shaped" form, whereby lines which can be assumed to be objectively straight and parallel are represented as arched. In the very common rendering of the throne in compositions of the seated Christ or the Virgin and Child, the objectively straight sides of the throne are rendered curved (Figure 3.4).

In these and many other images, pictorial space is curved – or rather, certain sections of it are curved – in a manner which is fundamentally different from that of Renaissance linear perspective. However, it would be incorrect to describe the space of the icon as Non-Euclidean in any strict, geometrical sense of the term, as such a space would follow the rules of Non-Euclidean geometry throughout the whole surface of the image. This is clearly not what happens here. So, not only could the medieval icon painter have not constructed pictorial space following the logic of Non-Euclidean geometry long before the invention of Non-Euclidean geometry, but also, even if we lost sight of the historical perspective, we would be unable to explain the complexity of the space of the icon by the rules deriving from Non-Euclidean geometry. At the same time, it is perfectly possible to have

Figure 3.2 *Mary Receiving the Purple*, Kariye Camii, Constantinople, ca. 1304, inner narthex, bay 3, West, wall lunette; permission by Dumbarton Oaks.

Figure 3.3 Reconstruction of the building to the viewer's left in Figure 3.2; my drawing.

Figure 3.4 Barrel-like deformations: (a) Novgorod School, thirteenth century, fragment from an icon; (b) twelfth century, fragment from a miniature; (c) Italian, thirteenth century; fragment from an icon (from Zhegin, see bibliography).

a spatial construction which is not that of Euclid, but does not conform to the rules of Non-Euclidean geometry either. A curved space does not necessarily imply Non-Euclidean geometry, as Tarabukin mentioned in his text.

The metaphor of Non-Euclidean geometry persisted, however, because it served so well the larger purpose at the heart of Russian critiques of the icon. Florensky pointedly kept using the term "Euclidean-Kantian space." In other words, while Dostoevsky's Ivan Karamazov took it for granted that a God-created world followed Euclidean laws, Florensky explicitly connected the Euclidean understanding of space to a modern, positivist worldview, which had excluded the presence of God in the world.

Conclusion and implications

This chapter drew attention to a concrete case study of Florensky's thinking which unfolded at the crossroads between religious faith and science-informed reason. More concretely, I looked at the little-known application of ideas deriving from Non-Euclidean geometry to Florensky's critique of the icon. There are several themes which have larger, theoretical implications.

Firstly, I put Florensky's utilization of the theme of Non-Euclidean geometry against the background of his project of developing a mathematical worldview, a notion going back to the Russian mathematician Nikolai Bugaev. The author's aim is clearly not to make a contribution to mathematics as such, but to use science in general and mathematics in particular to advance his brand of religious philosophy. The mathematical worldview was ultimately based on the idea of unity and was meant to counteract the fragmentariness of the analytical worldview at the heart of Western modernity. This idea forms the frame within which the discussion on Non-Euclidean geometry in icons takes place. More generally, it is revealing of Florensky's insistent concern with the relationship between faith and reason, which not only has an uninterrupted history in Christian thought, but also makes interesting points of contact with contemporary philosophy, which has engaged with the relationship between secular and religious reason. Philosophers such as Charles Taylor and others have demonstrated the need for thinking through the models of this relationship worked out in different intellectual traditions beyond the unique Western paradigm, which rests on the opposition between faith and reason. I am suggesting here that Russian religious philosophy represents one such model, which lies in the background of Florensky's intriguing recourse to Non-Euclidean geometry.

Secondly, I showed that in Russia, as in the West, there was a tradition, especially among the avant-garde, of applying the trope of Non-Euclidean geometry to non-scientific contexts in poetry, painting, etc. I claimed that there was a specifically Dostoevskian theme within this tradition which drew a connection between Non-Euclidean geometry and the problem of Christian belief in the modern world. Florensky's notion that space in the icon is a visual analogue of Non-Euclidean geometry was understood here as an original elaboration of this theme that ultimately goes back to Dostoevsky. According to this interpretation, in the Russian context, Non-Euclidean geometry was used as a metaphor that advanced the larger Russian critique of Western modernity. This view is very much in the spirit of Russian religious philosophy, much of which was formulated in a head-on

64 *The unity of faith and reason*

confrontation not only with modern Western philosophy, but with Kant's philosophy in particular.[30] Against this background, Non-Euclidean geometry became the banner of a Christian-Orthodox position, which advertised itself as a religious-philosophical alternative to Western philosophy and culture. In this way, Russian critiques of the icon became part of the larger Russian critique of Western modernity.

Notes

1 On the varying definitions of "reverse perspective," see Antonova, "On the Problem of 'Reverse Perspective,'" pp. 464–470. For more on Russian authors (Florensky, Zhegin, Uspensky), see Kemp and Antonova, "'Reverse Perspective'," pp. 399–433.
2 Florensky, "*Ob odnoi predpos'ilke mirovozreniia*" (On a Prerequisite of a Worldview), p. 7; my translation.
3 Demidov, "*O matematike v tvorchestvo P.A. Florenskogo*" (On Mathematics in the Works of P.A. Florensky), p. 171; my translation.
4 In a letter to his teacher, Egorov, Luzin described the effect that Florensky's *The Pillar and Ground of Truth* had had on him: "As I read it I was stunned the entire time by blows from a battering ram" (cited in Graham and Kantor, *Naming Infinity*, p. 83). Earlier, in 1908, he had written to Florensky: "I owe my interest in life to you" (cited *op. cit.*). See also, Charles Ford, "The Influence of P.A. Florensky on N.N. Luzin," *Historia Mathematica*, vol.25/3, 1998, pp. 332–339.
5 Luzin in a letter to his wife in the summer of 1908, cited in Graham and Kantor, *Naming Infinity*, p. 178.
6 Demidov and Ford, "On the Road to a Unified Worldview," p. 608.
7 Florensky's letter to his mother of 4 October 1900 cited in Demidov, "*O matematike v tvorchestvo P A. Florenskogo*" (On Mathematics in the Works of P.A. Florensky); my translation, p. 173.
8 Ibid.
9 See Nikolai Bugaev, "*Matematika i nauchno-filosofskogo mirovozzrenie*" (Mathematics and the Scientific-Philosophical Worldview), *Voprosy filosofii i psikhologii* (Questions of Philosophy and Psychology), book 5 (45) (Moscow, 1898), pp. 697–717.
10 See Graham and Kantor, *Naming Infinity*, pp. 18ff and Demidov and Ford, "On the Road to a Unified Worldview."
11 I have discussed this issue in some detail in my "Non-Euclidean Geometry in the Russian History of Art: On a Little-Known Application of a Scientific Theory," *Leonardo*, vol.51/5, 2019, pp. 1–11.
12 For a useful introduction to Non-Euclidean geometry, see Marvin Greenberg, *Euclidean and Non-Euclidean Geometries*, 3rd ed. (New York, 1993, first in 1974).
13 See Linda Henderson, "A New Facet of Cubism: The 'Fourth Dimension' and 'Non-Euclidean Geometry' Reinterpreted," *The Art Quarterly*, Winter 1971, pp. 410–433 and, in a much more extended form, in the book by the same author, *The Fourth Dimension and Non-Euclidean Geometry in Modern Art*, rev. ed. (Princeton, NJ: Princeton University Press, 1983, 2013). Also, Tom Gibbons, "Cubism and the 'Fourth Dimension' in the Context of Late Nineteenth-Century and Early Twentieth-Century Revival of Occult Idealism," *Journal of*

The unity of faith and reason 65

the Warburg and the Courtauld Institutes, vol.44, 1981, pp. 130–147 and Tony Robbin, *Shadows of Reality, the Fourth Dimension in Relativity, Cubism, and Modern Thought* (New Haven and London, 2006) and again, by Robbin, Tony, "The Fourth Dimension in Painting" in Assimina Kaniari and Marina Wallace (eds.), *Acts of Seeing: Artists, Scientists, and the History of the Visual: A Volume Dedicated to Martin Kemp* (London, 2009), pp. 87–102.

14 For the anti-Kantian stance of Russian philosophers, see Zakhar Kamenskii and V.A. Zhuchkov (eds.), *Kant i filosofiia v Rossii* (Kant and Philosophy in Russia) (Moscow, 1994).
15 The Italian mathematician Beltrami proved in 1886 exactly this (i.e. that Euclid's Postulate was impossible to prove).
16 The idea of a curved space came again to the fore in the 1920s with Einstein's General Relativity Theory, proposed in 1916 (the notion of the curvature of the space–time continuum was missing in the 1905 Special Theory).
17 See Khlebnikov's poem "Razin" in *Collected Works of Velimir Khlebnikov*, vol.3: *Selected Poems*, tr. Paul Schmidt (Cambridge, MA and London, 1997).
18 On the Dostoevskian tradition on Non-Euclidean geometry, see my " 'Daring to Think' of a Non-Euclidean World: Science and Religion in Russian Critiques of the Icon," *Sobornost*, vol.40/1, 2018, pp. 18–31.
19 Fyodor Dostoevsky, *The Brothers Karamazov* (1880) (Harmondsworth, ca. 1958).
20 Pavel Florensky, "*Analiz prostranstvennosti (i vremeni) v khudozestvenno-izobrazitel'nnikh proizvedeniiakh*" (Analysis of Space (and Time) in the Works of Visual Art) (written in 1924–25) in Pavel Florensky, *Istoriia i filosofiia iskusstva* (History and Philosophy of Art) (Moscow, 2000), p. 295; my translation.
21 Nikolai Tarabukin, "*Filosofiia ikony*" (The Philosophy of the Icon) (c. 1922–1923) MS, Rossiiskaia Gosudarstvennaia Biblioteka, Nauchno-issledovatel'skii otdel rukopisei, pp. 627, 60–61; my translation. Tellingly, Tarabukin makes references to Florensky's *Mnimosti v geometrii* (a text that does not mention Non-Euclidean geometry), which shows that he was well-familiar with Florensky's works.
22 Antonova, "On the Problem of 'Reverse Perspective,'" pp. 464–470. There is a glossary at the end of the article which briefly outlines the six definitions.
23 One of the three preconditions has to do with the vision of the beholder (a monocular vision from a privileged point of view and a fixed position), while the other two assume that the object of depiction is static and immobile and exclude the role of psycho-physiological processes such as memory.
24 Kemp and Antonova, " 'Reverse Perspective'," pp. 399–433.
25 Florensky, "Reverse Perspective," p. 265.
26 Ibid., p. 267; the original source by Mach has been lost.
27 Ibid.; from Ernst Makh, *Analiz oshchushenii* (Moscow, 1907), p. 354; Ernst Mach, *The Analysis of Sensations and the Relation of the Psychical to the Physical* (New York, 1959), p. 181.
28 See Florensky, "*Analiz*," p. 295.
29 Lev Zhegin, *Iazik zhivopisnogo proizvedeniia* (The Language of the Work of Art) (Moscow, 1970), p. 66.
30 See Kamenskii and Zhuchkov (eds.), *Kant i filosofiia v Rossii* (Kant and Philosophy in Russia).

4 The organic unity of the icon and the Church ritual as a synthesis of the arts

In this last chapter I draw attention to yet another adaptation of the concept of unity in Florensky's theory of the icon. In his 1918 essay, "The Church Ritual as a Synthesis of the Arts," Florensky insisted on the importance of understanding the icon in its organic unity with all other aspects of Church ritual (the lighting of the candles, the singing of the choir, the movement of the priests, etc.). This text was written in direct response to Bolshevik cultural policy on religious art in the aftermath of the October Revolution in 1917. In the first section, I interpret the new government's removal of religious art from churches and monasteries to museums and art galleries as a sustained iconoclastic attempt aimed at the suppression of the original, religious meaning of the work, even while preserving physically the work itself.

In the second section I consider Florensky's essay as an iconophile reaction, somewhat surprisingly formulated in organicist terms. The author believes that the icon belongs to a functioning church which fulfils the role of a "living museum" and a "laboratory" for the study of "the problem of religious art." The third section is organized around the attempt at drawing the deeper meaning of "the problem of religious art," which Florensky alludes to, but leaves unexamined. I show that the link between the inherent weakness of Western, Kantian aesthetics, on the one hand and the failure of the Western project of modernity on the other goes back to the German romantics, as well as makes points of contact with postmodern aesthetic theories.

Bolshevik cultural policy on religious art: iconoclasm as the destruction of meaning

In 2007, a scandal erupted among the Greek clergy in connection with the newly executed frescoes at a church in Kilkis in Northern Greece.[1] The iconographer, Costas Vafiadis (Konstantinos Vapheiadis), had included an unusual subject among his paintings, namely a portrait of Lenin, the leader

The organic unity of the icon and the ritual 67

of the October Revolution. Lenin was shown in the act of cutting the beard of St. Luke of the Crimea (1877–1961), who was balancing an icon in his hands, while another icon emerged from his pocket (Figure 4.1). St. Luke, a trained surgeon, had continued to practice medicine after he had been

Figure 4.1 Fresco by Costas Vafiadis. The image of late Russian leader Lenin (R) is painted on the wall of the Greek Orthodox church of the Holy Virgin in Axioupolis, northern Greece; Reuters/Griogoris Siamidis, 6 February 2007.

68 *The organic unity of the icon and the ritual*

ordained a priest. Repeatedly arrested by the Bolsheviks, he was known for always keeping an icon of the Virgin during his operations.

Some of the Greek clergy reacted angrily to the inclusion of Lenin in St. Luke's icon. What would come next? A priest asked, "what's to stop them from putting up Marilyn Monroe's pretty breasts?"[2] Eventually, the fresco was removed and Vafiadis had to paint over it with another image of the saint, this time excluding Lenin (the outline of Lenin's face from the initial drawing is still visible though). Those who had been upset and threatened legal action were quite right to point out that no such iconographical subject existed in the age-old canon. At the same time, one gets the impression that they might have missed something of the meaning of the Lenin image. In fact, there is a long Orthodox tradition of representing iconoclasts – i.e. those who destroyed, burned, and damaged holy icons as, for example, during the Iconoclastic controversy in Byzantium (8th–9th c.). The most famous example is probably the so-called Chludov Psalter, a Byzantine work from the ninth century, which was acquired in the 1800s by the Russian scholar Aleksei Chludov and is now housed in the State Historical Museum in Moscow.[3] There is a painting in the psalter, well-known among art historians and Byzantine scholars, of the Iconoclast Patriarch of Constantinople, John the Grammarian, rubbing out an icon of Christ with a sponge attached to a pole. The image in Kilkis plays on this theme. The pictorial motif of the icon presses the interpretation of Lenin and the Bolsheviks as iconoclasts. In addition, the cutting of the saint's beard refers to what is arguably one of the most memorable symbols of secularization in Russian history: the tax on beards, instituted by Peter the Great. The tax was part of the Tsar's programme for the modernization and Westernization of Russia. In other words, the Kilkis fresco places Lenin within a typically Russian tradition of secularization, which was frequently forced from the top. Here, I would like to look into these related ideas (iconoclasm, secularization, forced modernization, etc.) on the basis of Bolshevik cultural policy on religious art.

My main interest focuses on what might appear at first glance as a paradoxical strategy, employed in the first years after the Revolution, of the physical preservation of religious works alongside the intentional destruction of their original meaning. In the process, a host of pieces of religious art was removed from monasteries and churches and ended up in the recently nationalized art galleries and museums. This is how Andrey Rublev's *Old Testament Trinity* icon, probably Russia's most famous medieval image, found its way from the Lavra of the St. Trinity, the famous monastery by Moscow, to the Tretyakov Gallery, where it can be still seen. The professed desire for the protection and safe-keeping of works of art deemed of artistic and historical significance was, in many instances, pursued with a remarkable degree of success, as witnessed by the Soviet achievements in conservation techniques, which were acknowledged in the West.[4] At the same time, as I have mentioned in another piece, this strategy of re-contextualization is fundamentally iconoclastic in a special sense of the term.[5] Iconoclasm is understood as a philosophically motivated position on the nature of the image rather than a physical destruction of a group or groups of images. According to this understanding, iconoclasm is by no means averse to images as such but to the possibility that the image can represent God. As Alain Besançon has shown, for iconoclasts – those in Byzantium, in Islam, or with Calvin – the issue invariably centred on this problem.[6] In modern times, this understanding of the image has been revived by Hegel.[7] In this school of thought, iconoclasm represents the refusal to accept that a visual representation can "contain" the presence of what is represented.

For the Bolsheviks, the museum and the art gallery served perfectly their double aim – of preserving the actual work itself, while destroying its meaning as a cult object and turning it into an aesthetical piece. Thus, one set of connotations was suppressed and another one was imposed. Lenin and the Bolsheviks discovered nothing new when they employed a strategy of re-contextualization. After the French Revolution, special depots were created in Paris to hold artistic objects until it was determined which would be disposed of and which would be housed in the newly created public museums.[8] While this aspect of Soviet policy has not been as systematically studied as the French case, it can be noticed that, in important ways, Bolshevik Russia was recapitulating some of the attitudes of revolutionary France.[9]

It is, of course, undeniable that the Bolsheviks' rise to power – just as earlier in France – was accompanied by acts of iconoclasm in the narrow sense of the physical destruction of monuments associated with the previous regime. The decree issued on 12 April 1918 concerns the "demolition of monuments, erected in honour of the tsars and their servants and the creation of projects for monuments of the Russian Socialist Revolution." Some of the avant-garde enthusiastically welcomed this process, which they saw as a creation–destruction dualism and an unprecedented opening for originality and the breaking of artistic canons. One of the major representatives of the avant-garde, Kazimir Malevich, asked: "Do we need Rubens or the Cheops Pyramid? [. . .] Do we need temples to Christ [. . .] when the church dome is insignificant by comparison with any depot with millions of ferroconcrete beams?"[10] In a similar vein, a poem by Vladimir Kirillov proposes in obviously exaggerated terms that, "in the name of tomorrow we will burn Raphael, destroy the museum, and trample over Art."[11] It seems fortunate that this Nietzschean sentiment did not win the day and that Lenin in particular was far from sharing it. The demolition of tsarist monuments was

70 *The organic unity of the icon and the ritual*

most commonly carried out with the qualification that all those of artistic value should be preserved.

In general, Bolshevik cultural policy on religious art was an aspect of the Marxist-Leninist understanding of the role of religion in society. The new regime's view of religion as an "opium of the people" (an expression that both Marx and Lenin used) or a dark superstition, muddling the minds of people, seemed to find no better confirmation than popular attitudes towards holy images. In Russia, as in Western Europe, icons were invested with supernatural powers and were believed to cry, to shed blood, to cure the sick, etc. A holy figure or the figure of the Tsar was believed, in some way (sometimes quite literally), to be present in his/her image. One can imagine that the militant atheists among the Bolsheviks were none too happy when they received a curious letter from a remote village in Russia, in which the villagers dutifully asked for a portrait of "the new sovereign Revoljutsia."[12] With a population so overwhelmingly religious, the Bolsheviks set out on a programme of "enlightenment." Divesting images of their religious associations became a primary task for the new regime, a task which was, moreover, seen as part and parcel of the struggle against superstition and ignorance. The attempts to demonstrate "frauds" behind miraculous icons and relics were nothing new in Russian history. Peter the Great was known to have been fond of finding out the secret mechanisms on the back of icons which were responsible for their "tears" or "blood." This seemed to have failed to produce the expected result, but rather confirmed the idea of many that the Tsar was the Antichrist. The Bolsheviks do not appear to have been more successful when they uncovered "miraculously preserved" saints' bodies which turned out to be wax effigies.[13] The reaction of an old peasant, which he reported to an American visitor at the time, is quite revealing: "Our holy saints disappeared to heaven and substituted rags and straw for their relics when they found that their tombs were to be desecrated by nonbelievers. It was a great miracle."[14]

Florensky's iconophile project: on the "organic unity" of religious art

On an October day in 1918, quite an unlikely group of people were holding a conspiratorial meeting. It had become known that the Bolsheviks planned to perform a scientific examination of the relics of Russia's patron saint, Sergius of Radonezh. The relics were kept at the *Lavra*[15] of the Holy Trinity in Sergiev Posad, one of Russia's most important monasteries, which housed landmark works of religious art such as Andrei Rublev's *Old Testament Trinity* icon. For believers, such examinations, which were clearly part of an openly atheist propaganda, were deeply offensive and constituted nothing less than sacrilege. On the instructions of the Patriarch Tikhon, Florensky and some of his colleagues working for the short-lived Commission for the Preservation of the Monuments and Antiquities of the Lavra undertook the task of moving St. Sergius's head to a secret place for safe-keeping and substituting it with the head of a medieval prince. Under an oath of secrecy, this was done and the action remained undetected at the time.

The incident is revealing of the reactions of religiously minded intellectuals, as well as many common people, to Soviet cultural policy on religious art. All of a sudden, in the immediate aftermath of the Bolshevik Revolution, religious believers felt threatened from all sides by a militantly atheist government and responded in a variety of ways. This is the immediate background of Florensky's essay "The Church Ritual as a Synthesis of the Arts." Of course, the expression "the synthesis of the arts" also intentionally played on the German *Gesamtkunstwerk*, usually translated into English as "the total work of art."[16] The idea of the "total work of art," which unifies all the arts, went back to the German romantics (Lessing, Novalis, etc.). It was later popularized by the composer Richard Wagner in two essays of 1849: "Art and Revolution," in which Greek tragedy is held up as an example of a "total work," and "The Artwork of the Future," which talks about Wagner's own ideal. Wagner's ideas were the main source of inspiration behind various avant-garde projects towards "a synthesis of the arts" all over Europe, including Russia, where Vasilii Kandinsky was very much taken up with the idea.[17] Florensky's own motivation in referring to the notion of the "synthesis of the arts" is rather different. As his essay makes clear, he does not search for this ideal in the future or in the remote past of Antiquity. For him, it is the Christian ritual that is the realized ideal of a synthesis of the arts. In other words, once again, the implication is that what the avant-garde were striving for was already a well-known aspect in the Christian tradition.

There is, however, another, wider framework for his text which is much less known. Both the language and some of the ideas of Florensky's essay make direct points of contact with the writings of Nikolai Fedorov (1829–1903), a fascinating personality who exerted an important influence on religious thinkers in Russia. Fedorov, the founder of Cosmism, is mainly known for his ideas on the resurrection of the dead, physical immortality for all, the related idea of the colonialization of the cosmos, etc. These notions are interwoven, in frequently unexpected fashion, in his less known writings on art such as "The Museum, Its Meaning, and Mission" (mid 1880s) and "Art of Resemblance (or False Artistic Regeneration) and Art of Reality (of Real Resurrection)" (ca. 1890).[18] We find echoes of ideas from these pieces in Florensky's "The Church Ritual," most obviously in the comparison between the museum and the Church. In Fedorov's words, the "museum of the future," which would include a "laboratory" for the preservation and resurrection of every individual, is compared to a church. Florensky takes the idea of the museum-church, alongside with the organicist terminology which was common among the avant-garde as well,[19] and uses it as the organizing thesis of his essay. His overall aim was to offer a critique of the museum as a secularizing institution.

Florensky completely turns on its head the logic underlining the Bolsheviks' policy on religious art. For him, too, preservation is important, but it is the *meaning* of the work of art that is to be retained. This is so much so that the actual physical survival of the object becomes secondary. One may wonder about the practicality of what Florensky calls "a superb idea" of taking Antique sculptures out of the modern museum and into the open, "out of doors in the sunlight."[20] However, one cannot deny that the meaning of the statue would be fundamentally different depending on where it stands and its surrounding environment. In other words, the meaning of an image depends not only on its pictorial representation but also on conditions of reception. In this way, an opposition is developed. The sacred space of the church – not only in terms of architectural structure but in terms of all the conditions available in a functioning church – is opposed to the secular space of the art gallery and the modern museum. The former provides "the specific conditions" in which the icon can "live," while in the latter "it dies, or at least it enters a state of anabiosis."[21] At the same time, "a museum that functions autonomously is false and essentially pernicious to art."[22] Referring to an essay by the art historian Pavel Muratov, Florensky writes that objects "have no, or almost no, meaning outside the totality of the specific conditions of life." The work of art is an "organism" which requires "the completeness of the conditions essential to its existence."

Florensky's thesis is that the religious image can exist only in organic unity with its sacred landscape, which is provided by the music of the choir, the flickering light of the candles, the smoke of the incense, the movements of the priests – in short all the elements that make up Church ritual. It is in this sense that Church ritual is, quite literally, "a synthesis of the arts," a "whole organism" which involves all the senses: vision, smell, touch, etc. This is important, because experiencing the icon as part of Church ritual is what guarantees presence – a notion that had preoccupied Florensky for a long time. What is notable is that while in his earlier writings Florensky had resorted to theological language, in this piece he consistently uses modern organicist terminology. This is striking since the doctrine of presence in the sense of the presence of the prototype in the image is, after all, a theological doctrine. In another piece, I suggested that using an organicist terminology, deriving from the exact sciences, served a purely practical purpose.[23] It was not only more politically neutral, but could also convey better Florensky's main idea that religious art is not only a matter of the past but is a genuine, living element of a modern society. At the time I was not aware of Fedorov's writings, cited earlier, which I now believe to also lie in the background of this particular essay by Florensky.

The tone of Florensky's text is noticeably polemical and the author insists vehemently on the Lavra of the Trinity being preserved in its original condition. The Lavra becomes Florensky's case study for his project of the "*zhivogo muzeia*" (living museum).[24] It is proposed as a "laboratory for the study of the most essential problem of contemporary aesthetics," i.e. "the problem of religious art."[25] The icon as the supreme example of religious art needs its natural environment just as a living creature does. Florensky draws an analogy with the new zoo in Hamburg, where animals lived not in cages but in open spaces, designed to be as close as possible to their natural habitat.[26] This same principle applies to works of art. The icon, as a living organism, forms a whole with its environment, i.e. the Church. Once, however, it finds its place in the modern museum, the "whole" is disrupted. As "there is no reality outside the whole," in the gallery we no longer look at the Mother of God herself, but only at her picture.[27]

In short, while using organicist terminology, throughout his short text, Florensky subscribes to a typically iconophile understanding of the image, which he had defended, as we saw, in several earlier works. The continuity with his earlier works is especially notable the only time that he uses Platonic-Christian language: "In a church we stand face to face with the Platonic world of Ideas, in the museum we see not icons but merely caricatures of them."[28] Thus, the icon is defined, just as in earlier writings, in terms of a Platonic Idea.

The problem of religious art and a critique of modernity

I would now like to go back to what Florensky calls "the problem of religious art," an issue that he himself mentioned, but did not explicitly engage with in his essay. So what is the problem of religious art? What is problematic about it? The short answer that I propose here is that the mainstream of Western aesthetics, deriving from Kant and dominant at least till the 1960s simply fails to explain religious art. Now, the concept of aesthetics is intimately linked to the concept of modernity. As Hal Foster says, "the adventures of the aesthetic make up one of the great narratives of modernity,"[29] while Habermas draws attention to the idea that "the philosophical discourse on modernity [. . .] overlaps with the aesthetic discourse in manifold ways."[30] Therefore, a critique of aesthetics almost by definition implies a critique of the Western, secular modernity or what Habermas has called "the Enlightenment project." The view that modernity is essentially secular and the related notion that art is a separate, distinct field of experience are elements within the larger division between faith and knowledge and between secular and religious reason. These notions have been highly contested in the context of the crisis of modernity since the romantics and have been taken up with a new vigour.[31]

This is the larger framework within which, I believe, it makes sense to place Florensky's concern with "the problem of religious art." This concern was provoked by the iconoclastic Bolshevik policies on religious art, but it was also a much more general reaction to the shortcomings of Kantian aesthetics and the perceived failure of the Western project of modernity. If one consistently follows the position that art is an autonomous and independent field (independent, most importantly, with respect to religion) and the experience of it is distinct (especially with regard to the religious experience), then the very concept of religious art becomes meaningless. It is in this sense that Nietzsche says in *Human, All Too Human*, that "that species of art can never flourish again which – like *The Divine Comedy*, the paintings by Raphael, the frescoes of Michelangelo, Gothic cathedrals – presupposes not only a cosmic but a metaphysical significance in the objects of art."[32] Florensky's critique of the icon – bound as it is with a critique of secular reason and the project of modernity – is, in some important ways, antimodern in the same sense in which the positions of many of the romantics and Nietzsche were anti-modern. At the same time, it also makes some interesting contacts with postmodernism.

Let us look at this stage very briefly at Kantian aesthetics and, more concretely, at what has been called "the first moment"[33] of Kant's aesthetics or the notion that aesthetic judgement is disinterested. The notion of "aesthetic disinterestedness" goes back to eighteenth-century British writers such as Shaftesbury,[34] but it was Kant who popularized it. As it is well known, in his *Critique of Aesthetic Judgement* Kant defines the viewer of an artistic representation as "indifferent to the real existence of the object of this representation" and as playing no more than "the part of judge in matters of taste."[35] In another work, he goes back to this problem and writes:

> Pleasure, which is not necessarily bound up with the desire of the object and which, therefore, is at bottom not a pleasure in the existence of the object of representation, but clings to the representation only, may be called mere contemplative pleasure or satisfaction. The feeling of the latter kind of pleasure we call taste.[36]

This first moment of aesthetic experience is, indeed, of crucial importance. As Ernst Cassirer has noticed, "leaving out of the account the existence of the thing is precisely the characteristic and essential reality of aesthetic representation,"[37] while Israel Knox states that "in a sense, Kant builds his entire metaphysical aesthetic upon the basis" of "the doctrine of disinterestedness."[38] Formalism, which was dominant at least until the 1960s, pressed on the claim of disinterestedness.

On these terms, Kantian aesthetics would be quite unhelpful in providing a framework for understanding popular reactions to icons, which clearly have nothing to do with disinterestedness. The experience of a Christian believer before a religious image is intimately bound up exactly with the belief in the "real existence" of the object of the representation. More so, his/her interest can be understood as "pleasure obtained from the idea of the existence of an object"[39] (though "pleasure" is not quite the precise word here). The very terms on which visual experience has been postulated are questioned. In order to have visual experience, we need a seeing subject contemplating the seen object. Since at least Kepler and later in Cartesian philosophy, this has been interpreted as a split between subject and object. At the same time, the experience of the subject contemplating an image disclosing presence seems to revolve not only round the act of seeing but more significantly, around *being seen*. In a manner, the image "stares back."[40] It seems that a much more intimate and active interaction takes place when the viewer is faced with a *re-presentation* of the deity. Bruno Latour has made a useful distinction between re-presentation and representation in his thesis that in the Renaissance the latter mode superseded the former[41] or, in other words, the image was no longer seen as a container of presence.

In some of Heidegger's later writings, he discusses this problem explicitly in terms of presence – and, not surprisingly, his language sounds similar to Florensky's.[42] That the sculpture of a God "is not a portrait whose purpose is to make it easier to realize how the god looks, rather, it is a work that lets the god himself be present and thus *is* the god himself"[43] is another way of insisting, as Florensky had done, that in the icon we see the Mother of God, "not her picture." Florensky would have readily agreed with Heidegger's claim that "the work is a work, as long as the god had not fled from it"[44] and that art serves to "accomplish being"[45] and "unconcealedness."[46] Gadamer's notion of "picture magic" also plays on the idea of presence or what he calls "non-differentiation." As Gadamer said,

> if it is only at the beginning of the history of the picture, in its prehistory as it were, that we find picture magic, which depends on the identity and non-differentiation of the picture and what is pictured, still it does not mean that an increasingly differentiated consciousness that grows further and further away from magical identity can ever detach itself entirely from it.[47]

76 *The organic unity of the icon and the ritual*

Rather, he continues, "non-differentiation still remains an essential feature of all experience of pictures."[48] In other words, the response to the image is coloured by the ancient belief that the image is, in some manner, a container of the presence of the object of representation. The experience of religious art is very probably the most extreme example of this phenomenon. According to Gadamer, "only the religious picture shows the full ontological power of pictures [...] in it we see without doubt that a picture is not a copy of a copied being, but is in ontological communication with what is copied."[49]

Gadamer's term "picture magic" is rather unfortunate, as it could be misleading. After all, there are sophisticated notions of presence, which do not necessarily imply elements of magic. David Freedberg's *The Power of Images: Studies in the History and Theory of Response* (1989) is, therefore, useful as a refined elaboration of Gadamer's notion of "picture magic." Freedberg's thesis starts from a challenge against the very distinction between the "magical" or "religious" function of the image versus the "aesthetical" functions.[50] The response to image, in Freedberg's reading, is complex, and it includes the element of presence, which Kantian aesthetics has failed to account for. So long as presence is a vital component of our response to certain images, aesthetic judgement cannot be disinterested – and, according to Freedberg, "there is nothing in the history of response to suggest the possibility of complete disinterestedness."[51] Further, the attitude of a viewer before a religious image has little to do with a pure judgement of taste. As Gadamer has pointed out, "ritual and ceremony, all forms and expressions of religious observance that are already established, can be repeated again and again according to hallowed custom without anybody feeling it necessary to pass judgement upon them."[52]

Postmodernist challenges to Kantian aesthetics, which centre on the notion of presence, call into question not simply the concept of art, but specifically the concept of *religious* art. They naturally tend towards the notion of the "anti-aesthetic," which "signals that the very notion of the aesthetic, its network of ideas, is in question."[53] Just as with Florensky, while undermining the theory of aesthetics, postmodern philosophers get involved in an attack on the concept of modernity as well.

Conclusion

In this last chapter, I considered one more application of the concept of unity in Florensky's theory of the icon, namely his insistence that the religious image existed in a unity with all other aspects of the Orthodox Church ritual. Florensky defended this idea in his essay of 1918, "The Church Ritual as a Synthesis of the Arts." In the first section, I drew attention to the immediate historical background to which Florensky's text was very much

The organic unity of the icon and the ritual 77

a direct response. I showed that Bolshevik cultural policy on religious art was iconoclastic in a specific sense of the term, i.e. what was destroyed was the original religious meaning of the work (rather than the work itself).

In the second section, I interpreted Florensky's essay within a tradition of iconophile defence of the icon, presented, somewhat unexpectedly, by recourse to organicist terminology.

In the third section, I placed the emerging debate on the nature of the icon from the previous two sections within a larger theoretical framework. The problem of religious art grows out of a profound dissatisfaction with Kantian aesthetics, which fails to explain the religious image. The failure of aesthetics is tied to the perceived failure of the Western, Enlightenment project. Once again, we see how Florensky's engagement with questions of art and aesthetics develops against the background of a profound concern with the crisis of modernity.

Notes

1 I thank my friend Theodore Christchev for bringing this incident to my attention. See the Reuters article, "Church Painting of Lenin Sparks Greek Row," of 6 February 2007.
2 Cited in the Reuters article, "Church Painting of Lenin Sparks Greek Row," of 6 February 2007.
3 The classic study on the Psalter is Kathleen Corrigan, *Visual Polemics in Ninth-Century Byzantine Psalters* (Cambridge, UK, 1992). The Chludov Psalter is one of only three surviving Byzantine psalters of the ninth century.
4 On the occasion of the 1929–1930 exhibitions of Russian icons in England and Germany, Grabar described the Soviet scholars' approach to conservation. See Igor Grabar, "Scientific Restoration of Historic Works of Art" in Michael Farbman (ed.), *Masterpieces of Russian Painting* (London, 1930), pp. 95–109.
5 See Clemena Antonova, "Re-Contextualizing Holy Images in Early Soviet Russia: Florensky's Response to Lenin's *Plan for Monumental Propaganda*" in Uwe Fleckner (ed.), *Der Sturm der Bilder: Zerstörte und zerstörende Kunst von der Antike bis in die Gegenwart* (Berlin, 2011), pp. 101–119.
6 Alain Besançon, *The Forbidden Image: An Intellectual History of Iconoclasm* (Chicago and London, 2000).
7 This is what Hegel meant by saying that "artistic form is purely finite, and therefore, incommensurate with the infinite context it is meant to represent" (Georg F. Hegel, *Lectures on the Philosophy of World History* (Cambridge, 1975), p. 112.
8 Francis Haskell, "The Musée des Monuments Français" in his *History and Its Images* (New Haven and London, 1993), p. 237.
9 See ibid., pp. 236–253, also Stanley Idzerda, "Iconoclasm during the French Revolution," *The American Historical Review*, vol.1, 1954, pp. 13–26.
10 Kazimir Malevich, "On the Museum" (1919) in Arseny Zhilyaev (ed.), *Avant-Garde Museology* (Minneapolis, MN, 2015), p. 269. In the same essay, Malevich says that "one could feel more sorry about a screw breaking off than about the destruction of St. Basil's Cathedral" (p. 271).

78 *The organic unity of the icon and the ritual*

11 Cited in Orlando Figes, *Natasha's Dance: A Cultural History of Russia* (Harmondsworth, 2002), p. 450.
12 Bernard Pares, *A History of Russia*, rev. ed. (New York, 1953), p. 490.
13 Donald Treadgold notices that these practices seemed to have had "only a limited effect on the faithful" (see Donald Treadgold, *Twentieth Century Russia* (Boulder and San Francisco, 1987, first in 1981), p. 187; Fulop-Miller comments also on "the ineffectiveness of Bolshevik attacks," (see René Fulop-Miller, *The Mind and Face of Bolshevism: An Examination of Cultural Life in Soviet Russia* (New York, 1928, first in 1926), p. 350.
14 Richard Pipes, *Russia under the Bolshevik Regime* (New York, 1993), p. 346.
15 *Lavra* means a monastery which has received a special status.
16 For an overview, see David Roberts, *The Total Work of Art in European Modernism* (Cornell, 2011).
17 Nadia Podzemskaia has been doing interesting work on this aspect of Kandinsky's work. For example, see her "*La science de l'art à la GAXN et le projet théorique de Vassily Kandinsky*" (The Science of Art at GAKhN and Vasilii Kandisnky's Theoretical Project) in Nikolai Plotnikov and Nadia Podzemskaia (eds.), *Iazyk iskusstv. Gosudarstvennaia akademiia khudozhestevennikh nauk i russkaia esteticheskaia teoria 1920kh godov* (The Language of Art: The State Academy of Artistic Sciences and Russian Aesthetical Theory of the 1920s), vol.1, *Novoe literaturnoe obozrenie* (Moscow, 2017), pp. 44–78.
18 For an English translation, see Zhilyaev (ed.), *Avant-Garde Museology*.
19 Isabel Wünsche has done some excellent work on organicism among the Russian avant-garde. See her *The Organic School of the Russian Avant-Garde: Nature's Creative Principles* (Farnham, UK, 2015); "Organic Visions and Biological Models in Russian Avant-Garde Art" in Oliver Botar and Isabel Wünsche (eds.), *Biocentrism and Modernism* (Farnham, UK, 2011), pp. 127–152; and "Natural Phenomena and Universal Laws: The Organic School of the Russian Avant-Garde" in Paulina Kurc-Maj and Alexandra Jach (eds.), *Natural-Unnatural: Organicity and the Avant-Garde* (Lodz, 2017), pp. 185–206.
20 Florensky cites Pavel Muratov on this, who, in turn, referred to a project at the British Museum.
21 The term "anabiosis" means "a state of suspended animation or greatly reduced metabolism."
22 Pavel Florensky, "The Church Ritual as a Synthesis of the Arts" (1918) in Pavel Florensky (ed.), *Beyond Vision: Essays on the Perception of Art* (London, 2002), p. 102.
23 Antonova, "Re-Contextualizing Holy Images in Early Soviet Russia," pp. 101–119.
24 Ibid., p. 101.
25 Pavel Florensky, "The Church Ritual as a Synthesis of the Arts," p. 102.
26 Ibid.
27 Ibid.
28 Ibid., p. 108.
29 Hal Foster, "Postmodernism: A Preface" in Hal Foster (ed.), *The Anti-Aesthetic: Essays on Postmodern Culture*, 8th ed. (Seattle, 1983, 1993), p. XV.
30 Jürgen Habermas, *The Philosophical Discourse on Modernity* (Cambridge, MA, 1987), p. IX.
31 Among the most important texts on the relationship between religious and secular reason are the following: Taylor, *A Secular Age*; Jürgen Habermas, *Religion*

and *Rationality: Essays on Reason, God, and Modernity* (Oxford, 2001); Habermas and Ratzinger, *The Dialectics of Secularization*; Richard Rorty, "Religion as a Conversation-stopper," *Common Knowledge*, vol.3, 1994, pp. 1–6. Some other authors working on this problem are Veit Bader, Jose Casanova, Rajeev Bhargava, Tariq Modood.
32 Friedrich Nietzsche, *Human, All Too Human*, tr. R.J. Hollingdale (Cambridge, 1996), p. 102.
33 Israel Knox, *Aesthetical Theories of Kant, Hegel, and Schopenhauer* (New York and London, 1936), p. 23.
34 See Elizabeth Bohl, "Disinterestedness and the Denial of the Particular: Locke, Adam Smith, and the Subject of Aesthetics" in Paul Mattick (ed.), *Eighteenth-Century Aesthetics and the Reconstruction of Art* (Cambridge, 1993), pp. 16–52 and Jerome Stolnitz, "On the Origins of 'Aesthetic Disinterestedness'," *Journal of Aesthetics and Art Criticism*, vol.20, 1961–1962, pp. 131–143.
35 Immanuel Kant, *The Critique of Aesthetic Judgement*, tr. J.C. Meredith (Oxford, 1911), p. 43.
36 Immanuel Kant, *The Metaphysics of Ethics* (1796), tr. J.W. Semple (Edinburgh, 1886), p. 172.
37 Ernst Cassirer, *Kant's Life and Thought* (New Haven and London, 1981), p. 311.
38 Knox, *Aesthetical Theories*, pp. 23 and 24.
39 Ibid., p. 21.
40 I borrow James Elkins's expression from his *The Object Stares Back*.
41 Bruno Latour, "Opening One Eye while Closing the Other . . . A Note on Some Religious Paintings" in Gordon Fife and John Law (eds.), *Picturing Power: Visual Depiction and Social Relations* (London, 1988).
42 On the similarities, including in language, between Florensky and Heidegger, see Robert Slesinski, *Pavel Florensky: A Metaphysics of Love*, (Crestwood, New York, 1984), pp. 114–116 and my article, "'Beauty Will Save the World,'" pp. 52–53.
43 Martin Heidegger, *Poetry, Language, and Thought* (New York, 1971), p. 20.
44 Ibid., p. 43.
45 Ibid., p. 138.
46 Ibid., p. 56.
47 Hans-Georg Gadamer, *Truth and Method* (New York, 1975, first in German in 1960), p. 123.
48 Ibid.
49 Ibid., p. 126.
50 David Freedberg, *The Power of Images: Studies in the History and Theory of Response* (Chicago and London, 1989), p. XXII.
51 Ibid., p. 74.
52 Hans-Georg Gadamer, "Aesthetic and Religious Experience" in his *The Relevance of the Beautiful and Other Essays* (Cambridge, 1986, many rpts. since).
53 Foster, "Postmodernism: A Preface," p. XV.

Conclusion and implications

I feel that after going through this book even in a somewhat superficial way, any reader would have realized what this study is *not* about. It is emphatically not a book that aspires to make sense of Florensky across the wide range of his thought. It does not consider all or even the majority of the Russian writer's works, but only some of those that illustrate a concern with visual categories of thought. Further, it is certainly not a book about art history understood in the conventional sense of the word. Indeed, the book has attempted to bring across the idea that it is misleading to think of Florensky as an art historian. Moreover, I have noticed that Florensky is not even that useful for art historians, as so many of his ideas, seen with the prism of art history, are plainly wrong. Thus, "reverse perspective" is neither "reverse" nor "perspective"; space in the icon is not that of Non-Euclidean geometry, etc. These considerations bear repetition, mainly because there is a natural expectation that a theory of the icon would deal with matters of art history. There is also a further factor, which accounts for the tendency to think of Florensky as an art historian. When his work was, in a manner of speaking, "re-discovered" in Russia in the 1970s and later, as he became better known in the West, he was introduced mainly through his essay on "reverse perspective," which is frequently interpreted – wrongly, in my view – as an art historical text. One of the main points I have been making is that what Florensky wrote (frequently using art-historical terminology) was religious philosophy. As I have made clear, I believe that his religious philosophy was important and relevant to contemporary issues, while, as art history, his writings, are quite weak.

So, what is the subject of this book? The book is a study of Russian religious philosophy and, more specifically, a major movement within religious thought in Russia at the turn of the twentieth century that is known as *vseedinstvo* (which I have translated as "full unity" for reasons I explained in the introduction). The concern with Florensky was determined by my belief that he was one of the most important representatives within this strand of philosophy. My contention throughout this book has been that Florensky's philosophical project should be understood as firmly rooted in the tradition of thought which goes back to the Slavophile thinkers in the mid-nineteenth century and then, via Vladimir Soloviev at the end of the century, entered the philosophy of the brothers Trubetskoy, Bulgakov, Florensky himself, etc. At the same time, Florensky stands out among the rest of the *vseedintsy* in his consistent engagement with questions of visuality. I hope that my book has demonstrated that Florensky uses obviously visual categories such as "icon," "image," "symbol" (in the sense of "visual symbol"), "perspective" (in the sense of the organization of pictorial space), etc., as a way of conceptualizing religious-philosophical ideas that lie at the heart of the Russian full unity movement. Finally, this approach to philosophy through visuality was highly original in ways which, as I suggested at the beginning, draw bridges to contemporary debates on the "religious turn" and the "philosophical turn" in modern culture.

The material I have drawn on in this book is occasionally related to that in my previous *Space, Time, and Presence in the Icon: Seeing the World with the Eyes of God* (2010). At the same time, my main motivation and purpose are completely different. In my earlier work, the task I set myself was to understand, as much as I possibly could, the meaning and function of the medieval image at the time of its production. My question was: what was the meaning of the icon to medieval man, who, in the words of Umberto Eco, was striving to "see the world with the eyes of God"? In the present book, my interest is fundamentally different. The question which informs this work is: what is, if any, the value of Florensky's theory of the icon to our contemporary modernity? Can this theory contribute to the analysis of some of the most urgent questions in aesthetics and philosophy that we face now? To tackle these questions, my perspective shifted from a more narrow art-historical and theological focus on Florensky's writings on the medieval image to a wider, philosophical approach to these writings.

Each of the four chapters of the book was organized around one connotation of the religious-philosophical concept of full unity in Florensky's theory of the icon. I showed that these connotations, embedded as they are in Russian religious thought, also present continuities with the age-old tradition of Eastern Orthodox theology and, occasionally, with Platonic thought. Further, in all these cases, Florensky's use of "full unity" was interpreted in its relevance to modern problematics.

Thus, Chapter 1 looked at Florensky's interpretation of the visual image as symbol in the ancient meaning of the term (from *symballein* which means "to throw together, to unite"). For Florensky, the function of the icon lies in the possibility it opens for man (immanent) to unite with God (transcendent) through the divine energies (but not essence) residing in the holy image.

82 Conclusion and implications

The terminology of essence and energies derives directly from the theology of the fourteenth-century Byzantine archbishop, St. Gregory Palamas. It was applied by Florensky in the context of a contemporary event, i.e. the Name-Worshipping controversy at the beginning of the twentieth century. The definition of the icon as "energetic symbol," however, served a much wider purpose. It directly attacked Western philosophy and specifically the Kantian opposition between phenomenon (immanent) and noumenon (transcendent) and the Cartesian scopic regime, which opposed subject and object in the process of vision.

Chapter 2 draws attention to another meaning of "full unity" with Florensky, namely, the notion of the unity of the icon, achieved through the construction of pictorial space, known as "reverse perspective." The principle of organizing space in the icon can be interpreted along theological lines. It allows for man's imitation of divine "vision," while imitation (mimesis) is an aspect of the process of *theosis* or deification, a doctrine central to Eastern Orthodox Christianity. The purpose of *theosis* is the unity of man and God, and so we have here a further connotation of the concept of unity. Florensky's interest in pictorial space was initially provoked by contemporary Cubism and especially Picasso's early paintings, which could be seen in Moscow at the time. It became part of a much larger challenge to Renaissance linear perspective and the Cartesian worldview, which underlined it.

Chapter 3 plays on another meaning of "full unity," i.e., the unity of faith and reason, which underlined Florensky's "mathematical worldview." Florensky's use of the trope of Non-Euclidean geometry in his theory of the icon was interpreted as an illustration of this worldview. While Non-Euclidean geometry was a favourite idea among the avant-garde both in Russia and in the West at the time, in the Russian context it had a specifically religious sound to it, which highlighted the still relevant problem of religion in a secularized modernity. In this way, Florensky's "mathematical worldview" was developed in a conscious opposition to the Western analytical worldview, while the very notion of Non-Euclidean geometry was seen by Florensky and his contemporaries as a way of challenging Kant's philosophy.

In Chapter 4, the organizing concept of full unity is applied to the notion of the icon as existing in "organic" unity with all aspects of the church ritual. Florensky's essay on the topic is seen as part of the debate on the nature of the image and a reaction to the iconoclast policies on religious art of the new Bolshevik government right after the Revolution. The modern, organicist terminology should not obscure the spirit of Florensky's text under our attention, which belongs to a long line of iconophile, mostly Eastern Orthodox theological literature. At a deeper level, Florensky's defence of the icon is also an attack on Kantian aesthetics and, ultimately, of the Enlightenment project of modernity.

Conclusion and implications 83

There are certain approaches and several themes that cut across all the chapters. Firstly, Florensky's writings are always a reaction to contemporary events: the Name-Worshipping controversy, Picasso's early Cubist works (which could be seen in Moscow at the time), the metaphor of Non-Euclidean geometry circulating among the avant-garde, and Bolshevik cultural policy on religious art. These events served not only as the historical background for Florensky's texts, but were the direct provocation for these texts. This explains, in great part, the frequently polemic tone of the author. Secondly, the contemporary problems that the author identified were frequently analyzed by recourse to Eastern Orthodox theological ideas, which Florensky consistently modernized exactly by drawing their visual implications. Thus, in Chapter 1, St. Gregory Palamas's theology of divine essence and energy is borrowed for Florensky's notion of the "energetic" visual symbol. In Chapter 2, the interpretation of the significance of the doctrine of *theosis* is mine, following, in my view, quite faithfully the logic of Florensky's approach. The relationship between faith and reason is a well-known topic in Christian theology. Once again, in Chapter 3, we witnessed Florensky discussing this relationship through the prism of visuality. Florensky's defence of the image in Chapter 4 draws from a Byzantine and Eastern Orthodox iconophile theology of the icon, while, at the same time, it discusses the visual as an aspect of the "synthesis of the arts," a notion closely associated with the avant-garde at the turn of the twentieth century.

A theme – common to Florensky and all the *vseedintsy* – is the challenge to Western philosophy, which, with Florensky in particular, almost invariably, implicitly or explicitly, takes the form of a vehement criticism of Kant's philosophy in particular. Not surprisingly, it is Kant's opposition between the noumenon (transcendent) and the phenomenon (immanent) that Florensky takes issue with in Chapter 1, while, in Chapter 4, it is Kant's aesthetics and especially the Kantian doctrine of disinterested aesthetical experience, that, as I have suggested, is the butt of Florensky's attack. One suspects that Florensky is not always fair towards Kant, and much of his criticism seems to be based on an intentional misunderstanding. Kant, however, became useful for Russian religious philosophers every time they addressed what they believed were false oppositions in the mainstream of Western philosophy, such as the disjunction between subject and object in the process of vision (Chapter 2) and the opposition between faith and reason (Chapter 3).

Like many of his contemporaries, Florensky felt he was living through a "crisis of modernity." In this context, he re-sounded, sometimes without any acknowledgement, themes already raised in the nineteenth century by the German romantics. These themes, however, are, in a manner of speaking, "Christianized," as the roots of the crisis of modernity are seen as lying in the rupture between the modern age and its Christian foundations. Thus, Florensky offers a distinctly religious reading of the problems posed by the modern age.

One of the arguments of this book is that Florensky's preoccupation with religion is not backward-looking, but is part of a living, modern religious experience which directly confronts the problems of the modern age. It is, in this sense, that I have called his philosophy "a project of religious modernity." In simple words, he believed intensely and passionately that religion had a significant role to play in our modern age. This belief was at the heart of the whole movement of full unity. The ways in which it was formulated made it anti-institutional and largely anti-modern, yet postmodern. After all, the idea of the unity of religious faith and secular reason presupposes an embrace of both faith and reason. It is here that the *vseedintsy* stood so often at odds with the positions expressed by the Russian Orthodox Church. Strictly speaking, the religious revival at the beginning of the twentieth century was spearheaded by religious philosophers and thinkers who, wittingly or unwittingly, found themselves in opposition to ecclesiastical authorities. It was not by chance that Tolstoy, who had done so much to bring Christianity centre stage, was excommunicated by the Church. Florensky himself, who became a priest, never broke with the Church, but as we saw, he frequently held positions that had been condemned by the ecclesiastical authorities (for instance, on the issue of *imiaslavie*, discussed in Chapter 1).

At the same time, he and other members of the movement were motivated by a profound dissatisfaction with modernity understood as the classical modern project advanced by Enlightenment philosophers. The crisis of modernity was, therefore, experienced very much as the outcome of the failure of the Enlightenment. In this sense, the Russian project of full unity was put forward as an explicitly anti-modern critique of the Enlightenment and as a religious-philosophical alternative to the worldview promoted by the Enlightenment. The critique of the Enlightenment philosophical tradition is, in some cases, an early precursor of postmodern philosophy of a later date (as, for instance, in Heidegger's later writings on art, mentioned in Chapter 4), as well as of contemporary challenges to the classical theory of liberalism, which ultimately has its origins in the Enlightenment.

As might have been noticed, all chapters but one end with a section titled "conclusion and implications." The reason for this is that these sections provide, apart from the usual overview of the preceding text, indications of the wider significance of some of the major ideas in the chapter. At one level, I have shown ways in which well-established concepts and tendencies within the Russian philosophy of *vseedinstvo* – such as full unity, the quarrel with Kant and the admiration for Plato, the anxiety about the crisis of modernity and the re-sounding of Eastern Orthodox theological ideas, etc. – underline

Florensky's writings on the icon. On the other, I have pointed, however briefly, at the implications of these ideas for contemporary debates. In Chapter 4, the "implications" formed a separate section, "The problem of religious art and the critique of modernity," within the main body of the text and were, therefore, dropped from the conclusion.

Finally, as I mentioned at the very beginning, what makes the writings by Florensky that I have selected here of interest to me is exactly his bringing together of two themes that are usually kept apart: the importance of religion to modernity and the value of visuality. Florensky's early concern with the significance of religion *and* visuality can be useful to contemporary debates on "the religious turn" and "the pictorial turn," which are studied by scholars in different fields, largely in isolation from each other. I have suggested several contexts in which Florensky might be relevant. I fully realize that I have only made small steps along a road, which is, largely, almost completely unexplored. I hope that other scholars will continue along the way.

Bibliography

Cited works by Florensky (whenever there is a reliable English translation, the references are from this translation; in all other cases, the translation is mine):

"*Ob odnoi predposilke mirovozreniia*" (Of a Prerequisite of a Worldview) (1904), *Vesy*, number 9, 1904; rpt. in his *Sobranie sochineniia v cheterekh tomakh* (Collected Works in Four Volumes), vol.1 (Moscow, 1994), pp. 70–128.

"*O tipakh vozrastaniia*" (On the Types of Human Growth) (1906), *Bogoslovskii vestnik*, vol.7, 1906, pp. 1–39; rpt. in Florensky, Pavel, *Sobranie sochineniia v cheterekh tomakh* (Collected Works in Four Volumes), vol.1 (Moscow, 1994), pp. 281–317.

"*Obshchechelovecheskie korni idealizma*" (The Universal Human Roots of Idealism) (1909) in his *Sochineniia v cheterekh tomakh* (Collected Works in Four Volumes), vol.3/2 (Moscow, 1999), pp. 145–168.

"*Razum i dialektika*" (Reason and Dialectics) (1912) in Akulinin, *Filosofiia vseedinstva Ot V.S. Solovieva k P.A. Florenskomu* (The Philosophy of Full Unity: From V.S. Soloviev to P.A. Florensky) (Novosibirsk, 1990).

"*Imiaslavie kak filosofskaia predposilka*" (Name-Worshipping as a Philosophical Premise) (1913); rpt. in his *Sochineniia v chetirekh tomakh* (Works in Four Volumes), vol.3/1 (Moscow, 1999), pp. 252–363.

"*Primechaniia sviashchennika Pavla Florenskogo k stat'e arkhiepiskopa Nikona 'Velikoe izkushenie okolo sviateishego Imeni Bozhiia*" (1913), *Nachala*, number 1–4, 1995; rpt. Pavel Florensky, *Sochineniia v cheterekh tomakh* (Collected Works in Four Volumes), vol.3/1 (Moscow, 1994), pp. 299–344.

The Pillar and Ground of the Truth: An Essay in Orthodox Theodicy in Twelve Letters (1914), intro. Richard Gustafson, tr. Boris Jakim (Princeton, 1997, rpt. 2004).

Smisl' idealizma (The Meaning of Idealism) (1914) in his *Sochineniia v chetirekh tomakh* (Works in Four Volumes), vol.3 (Moscow, 1999).

"The Church Ritual as a Synthesis of the Arts" (1918) in Florensky, Pavel, *Beyond Vision: Essays on the Perception of Art*, intro. Nicoletta Misler, tr. Wendy Salmond (London, 2002), pp. 95–113.

"Reverse Perspective" (written in 1919, presented as a lecture in 1920) in Florensky, Pavel, *Beyond Vision: Essays on the Perception of Art*, intro. Nicoletta Misler, tr. Wendy Salmond (London, 2002), pp. 197–273.

Ikonostas (Iconostasis) (1922) in Florensky, Pavel, *Bogoslovskie trudy* (Theological Studies) (Moscow, 1972), rpt. in Florensky, Pavel, "*Ikonostas*" in his *Khristianstvo i kul'tura* (Christianity and Culture) (Moscow, 2001); English translation in Florensky, Pavel, *Iconostasis*, tr. Donald Sheelan and Olga Andrejev (Crestwood, New York, 1996, rpt. 2000).

Detiam moim (1923) (Moscow, 1992).

"*Analiz prostranstvennosti (i vremeni) v khudozestvenno-izobrazitel'nnikh proizvedeniiakh*" (Analysis of Space (and Time) in the Works of Visual Art) (Written in 1924–25) in Pavel Florensky, *Istoriia i filosofiia iskusstva* (History and Philosophy of Art) (Moscow, 2000).

"*Avtobiograficheskia statiia*" (Autobiographical Article) (1927) in *Entsiklopedicheskii slovar' Russkogo Bibliograficheskogo institute 'Granat'* (Encyclopaedic Dictionary of the Russian Bibliographical Institute "Granat"), vol.44 (Moscow, 1927).

Secondary literature

Abramov, Alexander, "*Otsenka filosofii Platona v russkoi idealisticheskoi filosofii*" (An Assessment of Plato's Philosophy in Russian Idealist Philosophy) in *Platon i ego epokha* (Plato and His Epoch) (Moscow, 1979), pp. 212–238.

Agadjanian, Alexander, "Breakthrough to Modernity, Apologia for Traditionalism: The Russian Orthodox View of Society and Culture in Comparative Perspective," *Religion, State, and Society*, vol.31, 2003.

Akulinin, Vladimir N., *Filosofiia vseedinstva: Ot V.S. Solovieva k P.A. Florenskomu* (The Philosophy of Full Unity: From V.S. Soloviev to P.A. Florensky) (Novosibirsk, 1990).

Alpatov, Mikhail, "*Iskusstvo Feofana Greka i uchenie isikhastov*" (The Art of Theophanes the Greek and the Teaching of the Hesychasts), *Vizantiisky vremennik*, vol.33, 1972, pp. 190–202.

Anneri, Shlomo and de-Shalit, Avner (eds.), *Communitarianism and Individualism* (Oxford, 1992).

Antonov, Lachezar, *The Critique of Monological Reason* (Blagoevgrad, 2011) (in Bulgarian).

Antonova, Clemena, "'Beauty Will Save the World:' The Revival of Romantic Theories of the Symbol in Pavel Florensky's Works," *Slavonica*, vol.4/1, 2008, pp. 44–56.

———, "Changing Perceptions of Pavel Florensky in Russian and Soviet Scholarship" in Oushakine, S. and Bradatan, C. (eds.), *In Marx's Shadow: Knowledge, Power, and Intellectuals in Eastern Europe and Russia* (Lanham: Lexington Books, 2010), pp. 73–95.

———, "On the Problem of 'Reverse Perspective': Definitions East and West," *Leonardo*, vol.43/5, 2010, pp. 464–470.

Bibliography

———, *Space, Time, and Presence in the Icon: Seeing the World with the Eyes of God* (Farnham, 2010).

———, "Re-Contextualizing Holy Images in Early Soviet Russia: Florensky's Response to Lenin's *Plan for Monumental Propaganda*" in Fleckner, U. (ed.), *Der Sturm der Bilder: Zerstörte und zertörende Kunst von der Antike bis in die Gegenwart* (Berlin, 2011), pp. 101–119.

———, "Visuality among Cubism, Iconography, and Theosophy: Pavel Florensky's Theory of the Icon," *Journal of Icon Studies*, vol.1, 2012.

———, "'Daring to Think' of a Non-Euclidean World: Science and Religion in Russian Critiques of the Icon," *Sobornost*, vol.40/1, 2018, pp. 18–31.

———, "The Icon and the Visual Arts at the Time of the Russian Religious Renaissance" in Pattison, G., Emerson, C. and Poole, R. (eds.), *The Oxford Handbook of Russian Religious Thought* (Oxford and New York, 2019), forthcoming.

———, "Non-Euclidean Geometry in the Russian History of Art: On a Little-Known Application of a Scientific Theory," *Leonardo*, vol.51/5, 2019, pp. 1–11.

Apuleius of Madaura, *Apuleius of Madauros: The Isis Book*, tr. J.G. Griffiths (Leiden, 1975).

Asad, Talal, *Genealogies of Religion: Discipline and Reasons of Power in Christianity and Islam* (Baltimore, 1993).

Barber, Charles, *Figure and Likeness: On the Limits of Representation in Byzantine Iconoclasm* (Princeton and Oxford, 2002).

Bell, Daniel, *Communitarianism and Its Critics* (Oxford, 1993).

Begbie, Jeremy, *Theology, Music, and Time* (Cambridge, 2000).

Berdyaev, Nikolai, "Pikasso," *Sofiia*, 1914, pp. 57–62.

———, "The Idea of Godmanhood in Vladimir Soloviev," *Perezvon*, number 7–8, 1925, pp. 180–182.

———, *The Russian Idea* (New York, 1948).

Berger, Peter, *The Social Reality of Religion* (London, 1980).

Berlin, Isaiah, "German Romanticism in St. Petersburg and Moscow" in his *Russian Thinkers* (1948, rpt. Harmondsworth, 1978), pp. 136–156.

Besançon, Alain, *The Forbidden Image: An Intellectual History of Iconoclasm* (Chicago and London, 2000).

Blond, Philip, *Post-Secular Philosophy: Between Philosophy and Theology* (London, 1998).

Bohl, Elizabeth, "Disinterestedness and the Denial of the Particular: Locke, Adam Smith, and the Subject of Aesthetics" in Mattick, Paul (ed.), *Eighteenth-Century Aesthetics and the Reconstruction of Art* (Cambridge, 1993), pp. 16–52.

Bonetskaia, Natalia, "Interview with N.K. Bonetskaia" in Schelhas, Johannes, "Florensky Today: Three Points of View," *Russian Studies in Philosophy*, vol.40/4, Spring 2002.

Bowden, Hugh, *Mystery Cults of the Ancient World* (London, 2010).

Bradshaw, David, *Aristotle East and West: Metaphysics and the Division of Christendom* (Cambridge, 2004).

Bruce, Steven, *Religion in the Modern World: From Cathedrals to Cults* (Oxford, 1996).

Bugaev, Nikolai, "*Matematika i nauchno-filosofskogo mirovozzrenie*" (Mathematics and the Scientific-Philosophical Worldview), *Voprosy filosofii i psikhologii* (Questions of Philosophy and Psychology), book 5 (45) (Moscow, 1898), pp. 697–717.

Bulgakov, Sergei, "*Trup krasoty*" (The Corpse of Beauty), *Russkaia misl'*, vol.8, 1915, pp. 91–106.

———, *Ikona i ikonopochitanie* (Icon and Icon-Worship) (Paris, 1931).

Bychkov, Viktor, *The Aesthetic Face of Being: Art in the Theology of Pavel Florensky* (Crestwood, New York, 1993).

Casanova, Jose, *Public Religions in the Modern World* (Chicago and London, 1994).

Cassirer, Ernst, *Kant's Life and Thought* (New Haven and London, 1981).

Chrestou, Panayiotis, "The Theology of Gregory Palamas" in his *An Introduction to the Study of the Church Fathers* (Rollinsford, NH, 2005).

Coates, Ruth, "Theosis in Early Twentieth-Century Russian Thought" in Pattison, George, Emerson, Caryl and Poole, Randall (eds.), *The Oxford Handbook of Russian Religious Thought*, forthcoming in 2019.

Coates, Ruth, *Deification in Russian Religious Thought: Between the Revolutions, 1905–1917* (Oxford and New York, 2019), forthcoming.

Cormack, Robin, *Painting the Soul* (London, 1997).

Corrigan, Kathleen, *Visual Polemics in Ninth-Century Byzantine Psalters* (Cambridge, UK, 1992).

Crowther, Paul, *How Pictures Complete Us: The Beautiful, the Sublime, and the Divine* (Stanford, 2016).

Dawkins, Richard, *The God Delusion* (London, 2006).

Demidov, Sergei, "*O matematike v tvorchestvo P.A. Florenskogo*" (On Mathematics in the Works of P.A. Florensky) in Hagemeister, Michael and Kauchtchtschwili, Nina (eds.), *Florensky i kul'tura ego vremeni* (Florensky and the Culture of His Time) (Marburg, 1995), pp. 171–185.

——— and Ford, Charles, "On the Road to a Unified Worldview: Priest P. Florensky – Theologian, Philosopher, and Scientist" in Koetsier, Teun and Bergmans, Luc (eds.), *Mathematics and the Divine: A Historical Study* (Amsterdam and London, 2005), pp. 545–613.

Dobbelaere, Karel, *Secularization: A Multi-Dimensional Concept* (Beverly Hills, CA, 1981).

Dostoevsky, Fyodor, *The Brothers Karamazov* (1880) (Harmondsworth, ca. 1958).

Drewery, Benjamin, *Origen and the Doctrine of Grace* (London, 1960).

Elkins, James, *The Object Stares Back: On the Nature of Seeing* (New York and London, 1996).

———, *On the Strange Place of Religion in Contemporary Art* (New York and London, 2004).

Fedorov, Vladimir, "Predislovie: Pavel Florensky kak missioner XXI veka" (Preface: Pavel Florensky as a Missionary of the Twenty-First Century) in *Pamiati Pavla Florenskogo* (In Memory of Pavel Florensky) (St. Petersburg, 2002), pp. 7–15.

Figes, Orlando, *Natasha's Dance: A Cultural History of Russia* (Harmondsworth, 2002).

Finlan, Stephen and Kharlamov, Vladimir (eds.), *Theosis: Deification in Christian Theology* (Princeton, 2006).

Florovsky, George, *Puti russkogo bogosloviia* (The Paths of Russian Theology) (Paris, 1937).

———, "St. Gregory Palamas and the Tradition of the Fathers," *Sobornost*, vol.4, 1961, pp. 165–176.

Ford, Charles, "The Influence of P.A. Florensky on N.N. Luzin," *Historia Mathematica*, vol.25/3, 1998, pp. 332–339.
Foster, Hal, "Postmodernism: A Preface" in Foster, H. (ed.), *The Anti-Aesthetic: Essays on Postmodern Culture*, 8th ed. (Seattle, 1983, 1993), pp. IX-3.
Freedberg, David, *The Power of Images: Studies in the History and Theory of Response* (Chicago and London, 1989).
Fulop-Miller, René, *The Mind and Face of Bolshevism: An Examination of Cultural Life in Soviet Russia* (New York, 1928, first in 1926).
Gadamer, Hans-Georg, *Truth and Method* (New York, 1975, first in German in 1960).
———, "Aesthetic and Religious Experience" in his *The Relevance of the Beautiful and Other Essays* (Cambridge, 1986, many rpts. since).
Georgi, Fadi, "The Vision of God as a Foretaste of the Eternal Life According to St. Gregory Palamas" in Tamcke, Martin (ed.), *Gotteserlebnis und Gotteslehre: Christliche und islamische Mystik im Orient* (Wiesbaden, 2010), pp. 174–186.
Gibbons, Tom, "Cubism and the 'Fourth Dimension' in the Context of Late Nineteenth-Century and Early Twentieth-Century Revival of Occult Idealism," *Journal of the Warburg and the Courtauld Institutes*, vol.44, 1981, pp. 130–147.
Goleizovsky, N.K., "*Isikhazm i russkaia zhivopis' XIV–XV vv*" (Hesychasm and Russian Painting of the Fourteenth and Fifteenth Centuries), *Vizantiisky vremennik*, vol.29, 1968, pp. 196–210.
Grabar, Igor, "Scientific Restoration of Historic Works of Art" in Farbman, Michael (ed.), *Masterpieces of Russian Painting* (London, 1930), pp. 95–109.
Graham, Loren and Kantor, Jean-Michel, *Naming Infinity: A True Story of Religious Mysticism and Mathematical Creativity* (Cambridge, MA and London, 2009).
Greenberg, Marvin, *Euclidean and Non-Euclidean Geometries*, 3rd ed. (New York, 1993, first in 1974).
Habermas, Jürgen, *The Philosophical Discourse on Modernity* (Cambridge, MA, 1987).
———, *Religion and Rationality: Essays on Reason, God, and Modernity* (Oxford, 2001).
———, "Religion in the Public Sphere," *European Journal of Philosophy*, vol.14/1, 2006, pp. 1–25.
——— and Ratzinger, Joseph, *The Dialectics of Secularization: On Reason and Religion* (San Francisco, 2005).
Hamburger, Jeffrey, "The Place of Theology in Medieval Art History" in Hamburger, Jeffrey (ed.), *The Mind's Eye: Art and Theological Argument in the Middle Ages* (Princeton, 2006).
Haskell, Francis, "The Musée des Monuments Français" in his *History and Its Images* (New Haven and London, 1993), pp. 236–252.
Heelas, Paul, Woodhead, Linda, et al., *The Spiritual Revolution* (Oxford, 2004).
Hegel, Georg F., *Lectures on the Philosophy of World History* (Cambridge, 1975).
———, *The Phenomenology of Spirit*, tr. A. Miller (Oxford, 1979).
Heidegger, Martin, *Poetry, Language, and Thought* (New York, 1971).
Henderson, Linda, "A New Facet of Cubism: The 'Fourth Dimension' and 'Non-Euclidean Geometry' Reinterpreted," *The Art Quarterly*, Winter 1971, pp. 410–433.

―――, *The Fourth Dimension and Non-Euclidean Geometry in Modern Art*, rev. ed. (Princeton, NJ: Princeton University Press, 1983, 2013).
Idzerda, Stanley, "Iconoclasm during the French Revolution," *The American Historical Review*, vol.1, 1954, pp. 13–26.
Ierodiakonou, Katerina, "The Anti-Logical Movement in the Fourteenth Century" in Ierodiakonou, Katerina (ed.), *Byzantine Philosophy and Its Sources* (Oxford, 2002), pp. 219–237.
Ingold, Felix Philipp (ed.), *Picasso in Russland* (Zurich, 1973).
Ivanovic, Filip, "Union with and Likeness to God: Deification According to Dionysius the Areopagite" in Edwards, Mark and Ene D-Vasilescu, Elena (eds.), *Visions of God and Ideas of Deification in Patristic Thought* (London and New York, 2017), pp. 118–157.
―――, "Images of Invisible Beauty in the Aesthetic Cosmology of Dionysius the Areopagite" in Bogdanovic, Jelena (ed.), *Perceptions of the Body and Sacred Space in Late Antiquity and Byzantium* (London and New York, 2018), pp. 11–23.
Jay, Martin, *Marxism and Totality* (Cambridge and Oxford, 1984).
John of Damascus, "The Orthodox Faith" in *Writings, Fathers of the Church*, vol.37, tr. F. Chase Jr. (Washington, 1958).
―――, *On the Divine Images* (Crestwood, New York, 1980).
Kamenskii, Zakhar and Zhuchkov, V.A. (eds.), *Kant i filosofiia v Rossii* (Kant and Philosophy in Russia) (Moscow, 1994).
Kant, Immanuel, *The Metaphysics of Ethics* (1796), tr. J.W. Semple (Edinburgh, 1886).
―――, *The Critique of Aesthetic Judgement*, tr. J.C. Meredith (Oxford, 1911).
Kemp, Martin, *Vizualization: The Nature Book of Art and Science* (Oxford and New York, 2001).
――― and Antonova, Clemena, "'Reverse Perspective': Historical Fallacies and an Alternative View" in Emmer, M. (ed.), *The Visual Mind II* (Cambridge, MA, 2005), pp. 399–433.
Kenworthy, Scott, *The Heart of Russia: Trinity-Sergius, Monasticism, and Society after 1825* (Washington and New York, 2010).
―――, "Archbishop Nikon (*Rozhdestvenskii*) and Pavel Florensky on Spiritual Experience, Theology, and the Name-Glorifiers Dispute" in Kornblatt, Judith and Michelson, Patrick (eds.), *Thinking Orthodox in Modern Russia: Culture, History, Context* (Madison, 2014), pp. 85–108.
Khlebnikov, Velimir, *Collected Works of Velimir Khlebnikov*, vol.3: *Selected Poems*, tr. Paul Schmidt (Cambridge, MA and London, 1997).
Khomiakov, Alexei and Kireevsky, Ivan, *On Spiritual Unity*, tr. and ed. B. Jakim and R. Bird (Hudson, New York, 1998).
Khoruzii, Sergei, "*Filosofii simvolizm P.A. Florenskogo i ego zhiznenie iztoki*" (P.A. Florensky's Philosophy of Symbolism and Its Living Sources) in Isupov, Konstantin (ed.), *P. A. Florenskij: Pro et contra* (St. Petersburg, 1996), pp. 525–528.
―――, "The Idea of Energy in the Moscow School of Christian Neo-Platonism" in Franz, Norbert, Hagemeister, Michael, and Haney, Frank (eds.), *Pavel Florenskij – Tradition und Moderne* (Frankfurt and Berlin, 2001), pp. 69–83.
Kierkegaard, Soren, *Concluding Unscientific Postscript* (1846) (London, 1945).

Kireevsky, Ivan, "On the Nature of European Culture and on Its Relationship to Russian Culture" (1852) in Khomiakov, Alexei and Kireevsky, Ivan, *On Spiritual Unity*, tr. and ed. B. Jakim and R. Bird (Hudson, New York, 1998), pp. 187–233.

———, "On the Necessity and Possibility of New Principles of Philosophy" in Khomiakov, Alexei and Kireevsky, Ivan (eds.), *On Spiritual Unity*, tr. and ed. B. Jakim and R. Bird (Hudson, New York, 1998), pp. 233–275.

Knox, Israel, *Aesthetical Theories of Kant, Hegel, and Schopenhauer* (New York and London, 1936).

Kostalevsky, Marina, *Dostoevsky and Soloviev: The Art of Integral Vision* (New Haven and London, 1997).

Kymlicka, Will, *Liberalism, Community, and Culture* (Oxford, 1989).

Latour, Bruno, "Opening One Eye While Closing the Other . . . A Note on Some Religious Paintings" in Fife, Gordon and Law, John (eds.), *Picturing Power: Visual Depiction and Social Relations* (London, 1988).

Lazarev, Viktor, *Feofan Grek i ego shkola* (Theophanes the Greek and His School) (Moscow, 1979).

Liddle, Henry, Scott, Robert, Jones, Henry S. and McKenzie, Roderick (eds.), *A Greek-English Lexicon*, 9th ed. (Oxford, 1925).

Linforth, Ivan, *The Arts of Orpheus* (Berkeley and Los Angeles, 1941).

Lossky, Nikolai, *History of Russian Philosophy* (London, 1950).

Lossky, Vladimir, *The Mystical Theology of the Eastern Church* (Cambridge, 1957).

———, *The Vision of God* (Clayton, WI, 1963).

———, *In the Image and Likeness of God* (Crestwood, New York, 1974).

Luckmann, Thomas, *Invisible Religion* (New York, 1967).

Mach, Ernst, *The Analysis of Sensations and the Relation of the Psychical to the Physical* (New York, 1959).

Maidansky, Andrei, "*Amor caucus*: Soloviev Draws Spinoza" in Obolevitch, Teresa and Rojek, Pawel (eds.), *Faith and Reason in Russian Thought* (Krakow, 2015), pp. 79–91.

Malevich, Kazimir, "On the Museum" (1919) in Zhilyaev, Arseny (ed.), *Avant-Garde Museology* (Minneapolis, MN, 2015), pp. 267–274.

Margalit, Avishai and Halbertal, Moshe, *Idolatry* (Cambridge, MA, 1992).

Martin, David, *The Religious and the Secular* (New York, 1969).

Mikhailov, Alexander, "*O. Pavel Florensky kak filosof granitsi*" (Fr. Pavel Florensky as a Philosopher of the Boundary), *Voprosi iskussvoznaniia*, number 4, 1994, pp. 33–72.

Milbank, John, *Theology and Social Theory: Beyond Secular Reason* (Oxford, 1990).

Miller, Arthur, *Einstein, Picasso: Space, Time, and the Beauty That Causes Havoc* (New York, 2001).

Misler, Nicoletta, "Toward an Exact Aesthetics: Pavel Florensky and the Russian Academy for Artistic Sciences" in Bowlt, John and Matich, Olga (eds.), *Laboratory of Dreams: The Russian Avant-Garde and Cultural Experiment* (Stanford, 1996), pp. 118–133.

———, "Florensky as an Art Historian" in Florensky, Pavel (ed.), *Beyond Vision: Essays on the Perception of Art*, ed. N. Misler (London, 2002), pp. 29–93.

Mitchell, W.J.T., *Picture Theory: Essays on Verbal and Visual Representation* (Chicago and London, 1994).

Nekrasova, Elena, "*Neosushtestvennii zamisel 1920-kh godov sozdaniia 'Symbolarium' (Slovaria simbolov) i ego pervii vipusk 'Tochka'* (The Unrealised Project of the 1920s for the Creation of 'Symbolarium' (Dictionary of Symbols) and Its First Issue 'Point'" in *Pamiatniki kul'tury. Novie otkritiia* (Monuments of Culture: New Discoveries) (Annual Publication, Leningrad, 1994), pp. 99–115.

Nietzsche, Friedrich, *Human, All Too Human*, tr. R.J. Hollingdale (Cambridge, 1996).

Orsini, G.N.G., "The Ancient Roots of a Modern Idea" in Rousseau, George S. (ed.), *Organic Form: The Life of an Idea* (London and Boston, 1972).

Paert, Irina, *Spiritual Elders: Charisma and Tradition in Russian Orthodoxy* (DeKalb, 2011).

Palamas, Gregory, "Confession of the Orthodox Faith" in Pelikan, Jaroslav and Hotchkiss, Valerie (eds.), *Creeds and Confessions of Faith in the Christian Tradition*, vol.1 (New York and London, 2003).

Panofsky, Erwin, *Gothic Architecture and Scholasticism* (Latrobe, PA, 1951, several rpts. since).

Papademetriou, George, *Introduction to St. Gregory Palamas* (New York, 1973).

Pares, Bernard, *A History of Russia*, rev. ed. (New York, 1953).

Pelikan, Jaroslav, *The Christian Tradition*, vol.2: *The Spirit of Eastern Christendom* (Chicago and London, 1974).

Peters, Francis E., *Greek Philosophical Terms: A Historical Lexicon* (New York, 1967).

Pipes, Richard, *Russia under the Bolshevik Regime* (New York, 1993).

Podzemskaia, Nadia, "*La science de l'art à la GAXN et le projet théorique de Vassily Kandinsky*" (The Science of Art at GAKhN and Vasilii Kandisnky's Theoretical Project) in Plotnikov, Nikolai and Podzemskaia, Nadia (eds.), *Iazyk iskusstv. Gosudarstvennaia akademiia khudozhestevennikh nauk i russkaia esteticheskaia teoria 1920kh godov* (The Language of Art: The State Academy of Artistic Sciences and Russian Aesthetical Theory of the 1920s), vol.1, *Novoe literaturnoe obozrenie* (Moscow, 2017), pp. 44–78.

Pseudo-Dionysius, *Pseudo-Dionysius: The Complete Works*, tr. Colm Luibheid (New York, 1987).

Pyman, Avril, *Pavel Florensky: A Quiet Genius: The Tragic and Extraordinary Life of Russia's Unknown da Vinci* (New York, 2010).

Robbin, Tony, *Shadows of Reality, the Fourth Dimension in Relativity, Cubism, and Modern Thought* (New Haven and London, 2006).

———, "The Fourth Dimension in Painting" in Kaniari, Assimina and Wallace, Marina (eds.), *Acts of Seeing: Artists, Scientists, and the History of the Visual: A Volume Dedicated to Martin Kemp* (London, 2009), pp. 87–102.

Roberts, David, *The Total Work of Art in European Modernism* (Cornell, 2011).

Rorty, Richard, "Religion as a Conversation-Stopper," *Common Knowledge*, vol.3, 1994, pp. 1–6.

Rusakov, Yuri and Bowlt, John, "Matisse in Russia in the Autumn of 1911," *The Burlington Magazine*, vol.117/866, 1975, pp. 284–291.

Russell, Norman, *The Doctrine of Deification in Greek Patristic Thought* (Oxford, 2004).

Schmemann, Alexander, *Ultimate Questions: An Anthology of Modern Russian Religious Thought* (London and Oxford, 1965).

Schneider, Christoph, "'Will the Truth Not Demand a Sacrifice from Us?' Reflections on Pavel A. Florensky's Idea of Truth as Antinomy in *The Pillar and Ground of Truth* (1914)," *Sobornost*, vol.34/2, 2013, pp. 34–51.

———, "Pavel A. Florensky: At the Boundary of Immanence and Transcendence" in Pattison, Goerge, Emerson, Caryl and Poole, Randall (eds.), *The Oxford Handbook of Russian Religious Thought* (forthcoming in 2019).

Schopenhauer, Arthur, *The World as Will and Idea* (London, 1883, rpt. 1964).

Slesinski, Robert, *Pavel Florensky: A Metaphysics of Love* (Crestwood, New York, 1984).

———, "The Metaphysics of Pan-Unity in P.A. Florensky: A Worldview" in Hagemeister, Michael and Kauchtchtschwili, Nina (eds.), *P.A. Florenskii i kul'tura ego vremeni* (P.A. Florensky and the Culture of His Time) (Marburg, 1995), pp. 467–475.

Smith, Jonathan Z., "A Matter of Class: Taxonomies of Religion," *Harvard Theological Review*, vol.894, 1996, pp. 387–403.

Soloviev, Vladimir, *Sobranie sochineniia* (Collected Works), 10 vols. (St. Petersburg, 1911–1914).

Stolnitz, Jerome, "On the Origins of 'Aesthetic Disinterestedness'," *Journal of Aesthetics and Art Criticism*, vol.20, 1961–1962, pp. 131–143.

Tarabukin, Nikolai, "*Filosofiia ikony*" (The Philosophy of the Icon) (c. 1922–1923) MS, Rossiiskaia Gosudarstvennaia Biblioteka, Nauchno-issledovatel'skii otdel rukopisei, pp. 627, 60–61.

Taylor, Charles, *A Secular Age* (Cambridge, MA and London, 2007).

———, "What Is Secularism?" in Levey, G. and Modood, T. (eds.), *Secularism, Religion, and Multicultural Citizenship* (Cambridge, 2009), pp. XI–XXIII.

Terras, Victor, "The Aesthetic Categories of *Ascent* and *Descent* in the Poetry of Viacheslav Ivanov," *Russian Poetics: Proceedings of the International Colloquium at UCLA, 22–24 September 1975, UCLA Slavic Studies*, number 4, pp. 393–409.

Tillich, Paul, *Art and Architecture* (New York, 1987).

Treadgold, Donald, *Twentieth Century Russia* (Boulder and San Francisco, 1987, first in 1981).

Troeltsch, Ernst, *The Social Teaching of the Christian Churches*, vols.1–2 (London, 1912, 1931; New York, 1960).

Trubetskoy, Evgeny, *Umozrenie v kraskakh: tri ocherka o russkoi ikone* (Contemplation in Colours: Three Articles on the Russian Icon) (Paris, 1965).

Uspensky, Boris, *The Semiotics of the Russian Icon* (Lisse, 1976).

Vasilenko, Leonid I., "*O magii i okkul'tizme v nasledii Pavla Florenskogo*" (On Magic and Occultism in the Heritage of Pavel Florensky), *Vestnik Sviato-Tikhonovskogo Gumanitarnogo uniersiteta*, vol.3, 2004, pp. 81–99.

Vezin, Anette and Vezin, Luc, *Kandinsky and der Blaue Reiter* (Paris, 1992).

Vries, Hent de, *Philosophy and the Turn to Religion* (Baltimore, 1999).

Ware, Kallistos, "God Hidden and Revealed: The Apophatic Way and the Essence-Energies Distinction," *Eastern Churches Review*, vol.7, 1975, pp. 125–136.

Whitehouse, Harvey and Martin, Luther H. (eds.), *Theorizing the Religious Past: Archaeology, History, and Cognition* (Walnut Creek, 2004).
Williams, Rowan, "The Philosophical Structures of Palamism," *Eastern Churches Review*, vol.9, 1977, pp. 27–44.
———, *Dostoevsky: Language, Faith, and Fiction* (Waco, TX, 2011).
Wolterstorff, Nicholas, *Art in Action: Toward a Christian Aesthetic* (Grand Rapids, 1980).
———, "The Religious Turn in Philosophy and Art" in Nagl, Ludwig (ed.), *Religion nach der Religionskritik* (Wien, 2003), pp. 273–283.
Wünsche, Isabel, "Organic Visions and Biological Models in Russian Avant-Garde Art" in Botar, O. and Wünsche, I. (eds.), *Biocentrism and Modernism* (Farnham, UK, 2011), pp. 127–152.
———, *The Organic School of the Russian Avant-Garde: Nature's Creative Principles* (Farnham, UK, 2015).
———, "Natural Phenomena and Universal Laws: The Organic School of the Russian Avant-Garde" in Kurc-Maj, P. and Jach, A. (eds.), *Natural-Unnatural: Organicity and the Avant-garde* (Lodz, 2017), pp. 185–206.
Yannaras, Christos, "The Distinction between Essence and Energy and Its Importance for Theology," *St. Vladimir's Theological Quarterly*, vol.19, 1975, pp. 232–245.
Zenkovsky, Vasilii, *A History of Russian Philosophy*, tr. G. Kline (New York and London, 1953).
Zernov, Nicholas, *The Russian Religious Renaissance of the Twentieth Century* (New York, 1963).
Zhegin, Lev, *Iazik zhivopisnogo proizvedeniia* (The Language of the Work of Art) (Moscow, 1970).

Index

aesthetic disinterestedness 74, 79, 94
aesthetics 11, 16, 17, 66, 73, 74, 75, 76, 77, 79, 81, 82, 83, 88, 92, 94
antinomy, antinomical 4, 28, 29, 34, 53, 94
apophatic theology 26, 31
avant-garde 2, 9, 17, 36, 41, 42, 50, 56, 57, 63, 69, 71, 72, 77, 78, 82, 83, 92, 95

Berdyaev, Nikolai 5, 50, 51, 88
Bolshevik 53, 66, 68, 69, 70, 71, 72, 74, 77, 78, 82, 83, 93
Bolyai, Janos 55
Bolzano, Bernard 54
Bugaev, Nikolai 54, 63, 64, 89
Bulgakov, Sergei 3, 5, 9, 11, 19, 24, 25, 30, 36, 37, 49, 50, 81, 89
Byzantine theology, Byzantine theologians 22, 32, 44

Cantor, Georg 54
Clement of Alexandria 46
Cosmism 71
Cubism, Cubist 16, 36, 37, 41, 42, 47, 49, 50, 64, 65, 82, 83, 88, 90, 91, 93
cultural policy 66, 68, 70, 71, 77, 83
curved space, curvature of space 52, 56, 57, 58, 62, 65

deification 16, 36, 43, 44, 45, 46, 47, 48, 50, 51, 82, 89, 91, 93; *see also* *theosis*
dialectical dogma, thought 28, 1, 2, 5, 6, 8, 9, 10, 11, 12, 17, 18, 19, 22, 23, 24, 27, 28, 29, 30, 31, 41, 43, 44, 46, 48, 50, 51, 52, 63, 65, 69, 79, 80, 81, 88, 89, 90, 91, 92, 93, 94
Dionysius the Areopagite (or Pseudo-Dionysius) 43, 46, 51, 91
disinterested aesthetic judgement 74, 79, 94; *see also* aesthetic disinterestedness
Dostoevsky, Fyodor 16, 17, 43, 48, 51, 57, 62, 63, 65, 89, 92, 95

Egorov, Dmitrii 17, 24, 32, 54, 64
energy, divine energies, energetic symbol 11, 15, 22, 23, 25, 26, 27, 30, 31, 32, 33, 34, 81, 82, 83, 91, 95
Enlightenment 7, 9, 13, 14, 32, 57, 70, 73, 77, 82, 84
Ern, Vladimir F. 24, 25
Euclid, Euclidean geometry 16, 55, 57, 58, 59, 60, 62, 63, 64, 65, 91

Fedorov, Nikolai 14, 21, 71, 73, 89
full unity 1, 2, 3, 5, 6, 7, 8, 9, 10, 11, 12, 15, 18, 19, 25, 26, 30, 31, 32, 36, 45, 48, 49, 52, 53, 54, 57, 80, 81, 82, 84, 86, 87; *see also* *vseedinstvo*

Gadamer, Hans-Georg 75, 76, 79, 90
German romantic philosophy, German romantics 2, 6, 18, 66, 71, 83
Goncharova, Natalia 37, 38
Grishchenko, Alexei 37, 41

Habermas, Jürgen 14, 15, 20, 21, 73, 78, 79, 90
Hegel, Georg Friedrich 7, 18, 69, 77, 79, 90, 92

98 Index

Heidegger, Martin 13, 75, 79, 84, 90
Hesychasm, Hesychast 24, 25, 27, 32, 33, 87, 90

iconoclast, iconoclastic 12, 28, 66, 68, 69, 74, 77, 82
iconophile 11, 22, 28, 66, 70, 73, 77, 82, 83
imiaslavie 23, 24, 25, 28, 84, 86; see also "Name-Worshippers, Name-Worshipping controversy
Ivanov, Viacheslav 30, 34, 51, 55, 91, 94

Jesus prayer 24, 29
John of Damascus 11, 20, 26, 47, 51, 91

Kandinsky, Vasilii 9, 16, 41, 50, 71, 78, 93, 94
Kant, Kantian 1, 16, 25, 55, 57, 58, 59, 62, 65, 66, 73, 74, 75, 76, 77, 79, 82, 83, 84, 89, 91, 92
Khlebnikov, Velimir 56, 65, 91
Khomiakov, Alexei 6, 18, 33, 91, 92
Kireevsky, Ivan 6, 18, 25, 33, 91, 92
Kolman, Ernst 53, 54

Lenin, Vladimir Ilich 34, 53, 66, 67, 68, 69, 70, 77, 88
Leonardo da Vinci 17
Lobachevsky, Nikolai 55, 56, 58
Losev, Alexei 24, 30
Lossky, Vladimir 17, 21, 25, 33, 43, 50, 92
Luzin, Nikolai 21, 53, 54, 64, 90

Mach, Ernst 59, 65, 92
Malevich, Kazimir 69, 77, 92
Maximus the Confessor 27, 46
Meyendorff, John 25
modernity 1, 2, 9, 12, 13, 14, 15, 21, 32, 52, 54, 63, 64, 66, 73, 74, 76, 77, 78, 79, 81, 82, 83, 84, 85, 87, 90
Moscow School of Mathematics 3, 17, 21, 24, 54
museum, museology 38, 58, 66, 68, 69, 71, 72, 73, 77, 78, 92

Name-Worshippers, Name-Worshipping controversy 3, 23, 25, 31, 54, 82, 83; *see also imiaslavie*

Nazianzus, Gregory 43
Neo-Platonism, Neo-Platonists 30, 34, 91
Nietzsche, Friedrich 2, 12, 13, 30, 69, 74, 79, 93
Non-Euclidean geometry, Non-Euclidean space 6, 9, 16, 52, 55, 56, 57, 58, 59, 60, 62, 63, 64, 65, 80, 82, 83, 88, 91

organicism, organicist 66, 72, 73, 77, 82, 78

Palamite, Palamism 15, 23, 25, 26, 27, 30, 31, 33, 34, 44, 95
perspective, perspectivism 1, 4, 10, 16, 19, 20, 21, 32, 37, 40, 42, 43, 47, 48, 49, 51, 52, 57, 58, 59, 60, 64, 65, 80, 81, 82, 87, 91
Peter the Great 68, 70
Picasso 36, 37, 41, 48, 49, 50, 82, 83, 91, 92
Plato, Platonic, Platonism 2, 4, 7, 18, 25, 30, 34, 42, 44, 45, 46, 49, 54, 73, 81, 84, 87, 91
Plotinus 10, 46
presence 2, 10, 15, 19, 20, 22, 25, 29, 31, 32, 47, 51, 63, 69, 72, 75, 76, 81, 88
Punin, Nikolai 41

reverse perspective 4, 10, 16, 19, 32, 37, 42, 47, 48, 49, 51, 52, 58, 59, 60, 64, 65, 80, 82, 87, 91
Riemann, Bernhard 55, 56, 58, 59
Rublev, Andrey 68, 70
Russian religious renaissance 3, 17, 50, 88, 95

Second Vatican Council (or Vatican II) 15
secular, secularism, secularization 2, 3, 8, 12, 13, 15, 16, 17, 20, 21, 52, 58, 63, 68, 72, 73, 74, 78, 79, 82, 84, 88, 89, 90, 92, 94
set theory, set 24, 54
Shchukin, Sergei 36, 37
Silver Age 2, 3, 7, 9
Slavophile philosophers, philosophy 5, 6, 7, 81
Soloviev, Vladimir 3, 5, 6, 7, 9, 11, 18, 43, 48, 51, 81, 86, 87, 88, 92, 94

Spinoza 7, 18, 92
St. Gregory Palamas 15, 23, 24, 25, 26, 27, 28, 30, 31, 33, 34, 35, 50, 82, 83, 89, 90
symbol, symbolism 2, 10, 15, 16, 18, 19, 22, 23, 26, 27, 28, 29, 31, 32, 34, 54, 56, 81, 82, 83, 87, 91, 93
synergy 30
"synthesis of the arts" 9, 16, 66, 71, 72, 76, 78, 83, 86

Tarabukin, Nikolai 41, 58, 60, 62, 65, 94
Taylor, Charles 13, 15, 17, 20, 21, 63, 78, 94

"theology through images" 12
theosis 16, 36, 43, 44, 45, 46, 47, 48, 49, 51, 82, 83, 89; *see also* deification
Tillich, Paul 13, 20, 21, 94
Tolstoy, Lev 84
Troeltsch, Ernst 50, 94
Trubetskoy, Evgeny 5, 11, 19, 94
Trubetskoy, Sergei 3, 5, 81

vseedinstvo 1, 3, 5, 80, 84; *see also* full unity

Wagner, Richard 9, 71

For Product Safety Concerns and Information please contact our EU representative GPSR@taylorandfrancis.com
Taylor & Francis Verlag GmbH, Kaufingerstraße 24, 80331 München, Germany

www.ingramcontent.com/pod-product-compliance
Lightning Source LLC
Chambersburg PA
CBHW070741230426
43669CB00014B/2528